THE REAL CEYLON

THE
REAL CEYLON

C. BROOKE ELLIOTT K.C.

NEW EDITION WITH MANY ILLUSTRATIONS

GYAN

Published by

GYAN

Gyan Publishing House
5, Ansari Road
Daryaganj, New Delhi-110002
Phone: 011-47034999, 9811692060
E-mail: books@gyanbooks.com

Distribution Network
gyanbooks.com
India, USA, Canada, UK, Australia, France

ISBN : 978-81-212-3939-4 (PB)
First Published, Colombo

2nd Impression 2020

Printed at: Gyan Press, Delhi.

The Real Ceylon
Author: C. Brooke Elliott K.C.

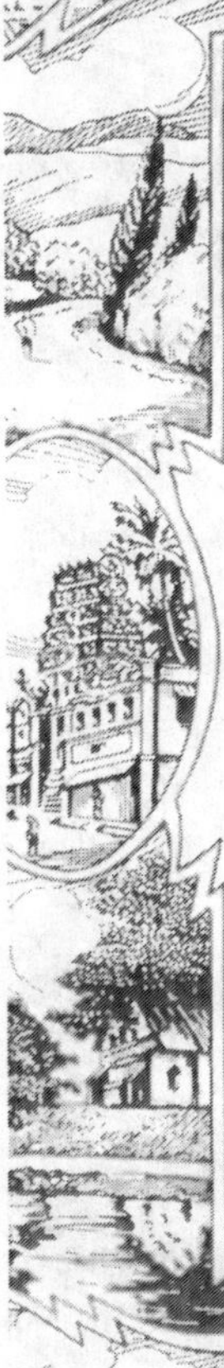

The Real Ceylon

C. Brooke Elliott. K.C. (Ceylon)

NEW EDITION
WITH MANY ILLUSTRATIONS

Printed by
H W CAVE & CO. in the Fort of Colombo

By courtesy *The Ceylon Tea Propaganda Board.*

A Low-country River Scene.

This Book is now dedicated

by gracious permission

to

LADY CALDECOTT.

Colombo,
March 21st, 1938.

FOREWORD

I

IN choosing my title I feel it may seem rather an arrogant one; but, when examined, it will be seen that exactly the opposite is the case. For I frankly admit that everybody, however young and wise, has a real Ceylon of his, or her, very own. Mine, as Belinda would say, is "just one of the ones." Anyhow after forty years in the Island one should have garnered a few vivid impressions worth recording in a quiet way in colours discreetly chosen from a literary paint-box.

Many gifted writers have written about a Ceylon that I, so far, have not been lucky, (or unlucky), enough to meet. Residents here need not expect much that is new, nor do they need visualisation; for if they just open their eyes — many don't — they can see all that I am trying to describe. But visitors to Ceylon may care to buy my experience for what it is worth Like Sam Weller and his knowledge of the public-houses of London, an Advocate in practice acquires knowledge that is extensive and peculiar. This little book merely suggests certain lines of thought, enquiry, and action, that many may find profitable and even amusing.

II

This is not a guide-book, or an Oriental Bradshaw, or a baby Encyclopædia Zeylanica; nor, incidentally, do I propose to give it away for nothing. It costs exactly one rupee, or one-and-sixpence in English money. It offers you the work of a plain person telling a plain tale; in which such comic-tragic characters as the Dhoby, the Resthouse Keeper, the Hired-Car Driver, and the Kitchen-Cooly — to name a few — will appear in the pursuit of their picturesque and unremunerative callings. Their quaint observations light up many a dark tropical day. One morning a wife forgot to administer his Sanatogen to her ailing husband. The Boy rebuked her later by saying, *"Please, why Lady sending Master to Office without sanitation?"* Recently, a Tamil cook applying for a situation, detailed his many culinary qualifications, and added simply, — *"P.S. Can give. if required, list of my mistresses."* On one occasion, in dislocated Tamil, I asked my chauffeur, Kumaran, how many gallons of petrol I had in my tank. He replied thoughtfully, *"Half-past-one gallons, Sir."*

III

My main theme is travel in Ceylon — where, how, and when to go. The book is, in fact, a topographical treatise conjugating the verb *TO GO* — Or, upon occasion, *NOT TO GO*. That word in Sinhalese is *palayan;* in Tamil, more incisively, *po*.

This little book is not, primarily, a commercial venture; but I felt that possibly a few advertisements might be helpful to newcomers of means and taste. It is believed that every practical or artistic want can be supplied by the firms and establishments represented. I except from the list, of course, the attractions of local law and medicine; as these learned professions do not advertise. Just in case however a sea-tossed traveller should arrive in Colombo suffering from *"heaviness of head or sneezing at the nose,"* I venture to mention that a certain Ayurvedic oil (unadvertised in these pages) might possibly be found remedial. It bears the attractive name of *Nethraloka Chintamini Thailaya*.

IV

In conclusion, permit me one generalisation; remember that Colombo is Ceylon only in the mercantile and political sense. The real Ceylon, as I see it, is found in the pale-green paddy-field with its threshing-floor upraised, while the thatched huts of the peasantry cluster under the coconut-trees on the high ground: in the white-robed worshippers on *poya* night bearing offerings to some little village temple; in the wastes of The Wanni; or on the sea-shore when the fishing-nets are hauled in, alive with struggling silvery fishes. Perhaps the most typical picture of all is the fragile watch-hut in a small *chena,* where by day and night man defends against the birds of the air and the beasts of the field his meagre crop of *Kurakkan,* upon which he and his skinny family are dependent, if something more than bare existence is to be enjoyed.

Now, let us cut the cackle, and come to the travel.

Thank you so much.

C. Brooke Elliott.

Outrigger Fishing Boat.

CHAPTER I

THIS ISLAND

Set in the silver sea........

THE first Question that arises is — What is Ceylon? second, What is Travel? The former is easy, the latter somewhat difficult to define. Ceylon is a pear-shaped Island roughly about the size of Ireland, 25,332 square miles in extent. It is 270 miles from North to South, and 140 miles from East to West at the broadest part. Ceylon has many names — Taprobane, and Lanka, being the best known.

Travel, according to the learned Mr. Webster, means *"to go on foot..............to pass by riding in any manner to a distant place...............to pass, to go, to move,"* which is interesting: but wrong. For in Ceylon to-day few people ever ride, fewer walk, and nothing ever moves unless compelled.

Apparently from what one sees the generally accepted idea of travel to-day is to execute a hurried round of heated sight-seeing according to preordained plan. Whereas, of course, the only true conception of travel is not to know where you are going; and then get there. That is why Columbus was so pleased with America.

Concerning Ceylon in general, there are four periods of Ceylon history — to adopt a very rough classification. First comes the immense period prior to the Portuguese occupation. The second is the Portuguese Era. Thirdly we have the Dutch. And lastly the British. This is no place to attempt, even briefly, to touch on prehistoric Ceylon and its history during the Dark and Middle Ages. A little book by Mr. Donald Obeyesekere is helpful, while the *Mahawansa* and other Sinhalese records give full accounts of the rise and fall, the ebb and flow, of Tamil and Sinhalese dynasties. The first period gave us the Buried Cities; the Portuguese imported Roman Catholicism; the Dutch provided our Common Law; and the British gave Ceylon Peace and Prosperity.

The Portuguese Era has been lengthily reviewed by Dr. Pieris. I am not aware of any wholly satisfactory work on Dutch Times, but a very charming little pamphlet by Mr. R. G. Anthonisz, late Archivist to the Government of Ceylon, entitled

"THE DUTCH IN CEYLON"

gives one a vivid and pleasing glimpse of their life and times. We shall often have Dutch happenings revealed to us in our future wanderings throughout the Island.

A few statistics may be quoted here. I am much indebted to the Registrar-General who has very kindly furnished the following information :—

I.—POPULATION BY RACE *

Race		Estimated Population 1931.	Estd. Population 1936.
Europeans	...	9,153	10,200
Burghers & Eurasians		32,315	36.800
Sinhalese	...	3,473,030	3,775,500
Tamils	...	1,417,477	1,402,100
Moors	...	325,913	356,700
Malays	...	15,977	16,800
Others	...	32,564	33.100
Race unspecified	...	442	—
Total (Ceylon)	...	5,306,871	5,631,200

The history of a country is best sought and found in its public and private records; Ceylon is rich in such sources — still largely untapped. The Government Archives run from 1640-1796 in Portuguese and Dutch. Only a few Portuguese documents still remain. The earliest Dutch document is a minute of the Political Council of March 12th, 1640. Seven thousand volumes of Dutch records still remain to be translated — a task being undertaken by a Dutch lady expert.

* An accurate estimate of the race composition of the population of Ceylon is not available, as race statistics were collected at the Census of 1931 only in Colombo Town and on Estates. The figures shown above are based on the race distribution at the Census of 1921. The estimated population of 1936 is also calculated in the same manner. The accuracy of the figures therefore is not guaranteed. These are only approximate.

It may here be noted that 1640 was the date when Fort St. George in Madras was built and occupied by the British. From then till 1796 Madras and Colombo fought one another for supremacy — England *versus* Holland. England won. She had recently defeated the French in South India at the battle of Wandiwash.

Ceylon Records are stored in charge of the Government Archivist in the Secretariat on Galle Face, behind the State Council building. By the Archivist and his Staff I have been courteously furnished with much valuable information and he would, no doubt, welcome any traveller whose trail lay along archivistic lines. Much of this immense quantity of matter, amounting to seven thousand bound volumes, is largely unexplored. The judicial records are of pious and legal interest — one especially, dealing with a case of divorce. And the so-called "memories," that is memoranda of retiring Governors and other high officials addressed to their successors in office, are of peculiar political interest.

The Dutch records may be roughly divided — like ancient Gaul — into three parts, namely, the Galle Records, the Proceedings of the Political Council, and the General Records of the central seat of Government. While other documents such as wills, *thombos* (land registers), family *thombos* and parish registers, are of social interest. Further, there are nearly 1,000 volumes which are as yet unclassified. So this office is an ideal place in which to spend many a wet afternoon — provided one can decipher the MSS. and understand Dutch as written in Ceylon in the 18th Century.

Here you can see the sign-manual of a great Warrior-King of Ceylon, Raja Singha II, who flourished in the 17th Century and was an important factor in the history of Ceylon, with his Capital at Kandy.

The first Sinhalese King of Ceylon was Wijaya, who flourished about 500 B.C. and the Wijayan kings lasted till about A.D. 300; but there were invasions from South India and dynastic dissensions and interruptions. Probably the peak of this civilisation was reached at Anuradhapura about the time of King Dutugemunu A.D. 200. In those early ages Ceylon was known to the Greeks and Romans, and commerce with them was carried on by Arabs in dhows. In A.D. 413 a Chinese monk, Fa-Hien, visited Ceylon and wrote the inevitable book. But as he was a scholar and spent two years in Ceylon in search of Buddhist manuscripts he is entitled to a respectful hearing. He writes with charm. His work has been translated by Dr. Legge. I shall refer to him again later on.

From A.D. 300 a number of kings in different capitals strove for mastery; while various Tamil princes from South India invaded Ceylon. One Sinhalese King Parakrama Bahu (1153-1186) reigned gloriously and defeated the invaders. Polonnaruwa owed much to him; a fine rock statue still gives a royal impression of His Majesty. In A.D. 1232 the Sinhalese Capital was moved to Dombadeniya; then to Yapahu in 1270, to Kornegalle in 1350, and to Kotta near Colombo in the 15th Century. This shows the glorious uncertainty of a throne in those days.

At some period, not accurately ascertained and for causes as yet unknown, the great cities of the North-Central Province were abandoned gradually and fell into decay, to be swallowed up by jungle-tide. One cause suggested is malaria. Quickly, the forest grew up, overthrew dagaba, temple, and palace, and buried what was still standing in a vast leafy grave. Hence we get the "Buried Cities" — that were rediscovered in the 'forties of last century, and were gradually delivered by Government from the thraldom of the jungle.

We now come to the arrival of the Portuguese and the European struggle for supremacy that ensued for roughly three hundred years.

The late Mr. P. Narayanaswamy, a Colombo lawyer gifted with unusual powers of compression, once wrote and published a history of the world in 27 pages. Less ambitious, I shall briefly sketch the rise and fall of, first, the Portuguese and then the Dutch supremacy in Ceylon.

The strategic value of this Island was clearly seen by both nations in their scheme of Eastern Empire. The struggle for supremacy was vastly interesting, for in it we find the eternal triangle — the inhabitants of Ceylon forming the base.

The Portuguese were in the East nearly a century before the Dutch. More by accident than by design they chanced to make Ceylon. It was in 1505 that Lorenzo D'Almeida sailed with three ships to the Maldive Islands, (some four hundred miles south-west of Ceylon), in order to cut off some Arab merchantmen from Malacca. D'Almeida was however carried northward by currents and was the first Portuguese to set foot in Ceylon. No attempt whatever was made to annex any part of it to Portugal. Later in 1518, Lope Soarez d'Albergaria despatched a fleet to conquer Ceylon, which was then ruled by a number of Rajas, some Sinhalese, others Tamils, but all subordinate more or less to King Parakrama Bahu IX, whose Capital was at Kotta.

The main object of the expedition was of course commercial; to obtain supplies of precious stones, pearls, pepper, arecanuts, and, above all, cinnamon — *"The bride round whom they all danced in Ceylon."* No doubt too they had biblical visions of ivory, apes, and peacocks.

Gradually the Portuguese built forts as they obtained control of the chief ports, and thus were able to form a virtual trade monopoly. In this way they linked up Ceylon with Goa, the centre of their settlements in the Malabar Coast.

I have no space to follow the interesting story of the struggle between Portuguese and Sinhalese. Wars and rumours of wars tell a sad tale. For these I must refer you to books like Rebeiro's *History of Ceilão* by Dr. Paul Pieris, or Queiros' *Conquest of Ceylon*. Dr. Pieris has written a treatise in two volumes on the Portuguese Era, which is full of interest and scholarly.

Obviously Ceylon was a prize worth fighting for, and in 1601 the Dutchman Joris van Spilbergh sailed from Holland with three ships to open up trade relations with Ceylon. He started on May 5th, reached Table Bay on November 29th, and finally, after passing Point-de-Galle, reached Batticaloa on the East Coast of Ceylon on May 31st, 1602.

Then began the triangular struggle, already referred to, which ended in the ousting of the Portuguese in the course of a few years. By the year 1658 the Portuguese were finally expelled.

And then with the advent of the British, the Dutch were in turn driven out. And for the first time probably since the world began, in the year 1796 Ceylon entered on a long era of peace.

CHAPTER II

COLOMBO

CEYLON is the Tropical Paradise of the playboy and play-girl of the whole world. It has something for everyone; and everything — for some of us. No other island has such constant and lovely variety for eye, ear, and nose — though some of the scents are almost oppressively sweet to Europeans, as in the darkened flower-stalls of the Kandyan Temple.

Ceylon has been changing, is changing, and will continue to change; yet her charm persists. So far as I am concerned, I hope to serve the Ceylon, that I love so well, by describing some of her priceless possessions of the past and present — many ot which are in danger owing to what is sometimes called modern progress. Happily in the tropics, Nature heals ugly scars with jungle-plaster quickly; and in due season we may hope that engineers will no longer be encouraged to desecrate lovely lands-capes with concrete horrors, such as poles and wires over a small trout-stream — as has been done in the winding Kandapola Valley. Petrol pictorial pumpous abominations still disfigure some towns and even villages; and will continue to do so, till a Director of one of these concerns has been publicly and painfully boiled in crude oil. Vandalism is trying to rear its ugly head in our midst, though happily our public men are at last beginning to realise that beauty is not only truth, but also good business. I am reminded in this connection of the child who said — *"Why is it always easier to be ugly than pretty?"*

Best of all, the cruel and senseless slaughter, in and out of season, of game is being firmly checked at last; and sanctuaries have been established by Government, where beasts and birds can thrive and multiply. This is quite in accordance with Sinha-lese tradition, which is opposed to all taking of life: and public opinion is slowly coming to realise that the fowls of the air, the beasts of the forests, and the lilies of the field, are spiritual necessities in a highly mechanised age. If you come with me one day down the jungle-bounded valley of the Bul'ela, I will show you stainless arum lilies beside the crystal stream, and you will recall the voice of One who said:—

> *"Consider the lilies of the field, how they grow: they toil not, neither do they spin: and yet I say unto you that even Solomon in all his glory was not arrayed like one of these."*

II

No one, to my knowledge, has yet written a treatise on the Inns of the Middle East, which are the Royal Exchanges of Travel and Good-fellowship. The fine big old-Asiatic word for Inn was *Caravanserai* — which calls up a picture of a huge stone-built semi-fortified mansion, within which the Pilgrim or Traveller found refuge for himself, his beasts of burden, and his goods; and goodly provision of food and provender.

Hotels were introduced in the 18th Century into India, and we read in the *Bengal Gazette* of 1750 of a famous House of Entertainment, pleasantly called *The Harmonic Tavern.* It was described as *"The resort of the cream of Calcutta Society, where profligacy could be found tuning the lute."*

In Ceylon the tired traveller seeks refreshment and entertainment in Hotels in the towns, and in the Rest-houses scattered throughout the Island, some 120 in number.

Colombo is splendidly supplied to welcome travellers. On landing you are faced and graced by the Grand Oriental Hotel, in local Richshawdom known as "The *periya* (big) Hotel." A stone near the entrance tells us that:—

IN THE REIGN OF KING WILLIAM IV.
THIS BARRACK
Being the first of the Improvements in the Military
Buildings throughout Ceylon.
For which £30,000 was granted by His Majesty's Govt. in 1835.
Was commenced on the 23rd February 1837.
And
Was completed on the 27th October 1837.
When
THE RT. HON. SIR ROBERT WILMOT HORTON BART. G.C.H.
Was
GOVERNOR OF THE ISLAND;
And When
THE HON. MAJR.-GEN. SIR JOHN WILSON K.C.B.
COMMANDED HIS MAJESTY'S FORCES.

The names of Sir John Grinlinton, a Crimean veteran, and Mr. W. S. T. Saunders of Dickoya, figure honourably as the early creators of this famous establishment.

About a mile-and-a-half away, facing the green promenade called Galle Face, stands the Galle Face Hotel — so widely known throughout the world. Bound up with the Galle Face is the name of Shakspeare (Walter, not William). Delightfully situated on the foam-fringed shore of the green-blue Indian Ocean, with a huge open-air sea-water bath, this great establishment gaily caters for every taste and purse.

At sight of that swimming-pool, it is inevitably a moment —

When all agree
With one consent to plunge into the sea.

Seven miles away on the famous cabook hill above the sea stands the stately Mount Lavinia Hotel, where for so long the portly Mr. Link produced his famous turtle-soup for the fish-tiffin on Sunday. Excellent and safe sea-bathing is obtainable.

If you wish to film sunsets in colour, I recommend three sites — the roof of the Grand Oriental Hotel, the lawn of the Galle Face Hotel, and the garden at Mount Lavinia Hotel. I have thus secured marvellous sunsets, such as only Ceylon can produce. You can, too, in these surroundings conveniently slake the thirst that tropical sunsets usually provoke.

If I had to name a "Honeymoon Hotel" in Ceylon, I should say, "go to The Mount, my children!" Once, after a long illness, I recovered my strength rapidly staying at this delightful Hotel.

Now let us explore the Fort.

I might here, perhaps, explain that everybody in Ceylon talks about the centre of the city of Colombo as "The Fort." In the olden days it was a fine Fort, with high walls, a moat, and gun-filled bastions with a clear line of fire on the land side in case of attack. The original Fort of Colombo — like the original Fort of St. George in Madras was a modest affair — a kind of glorified stockade: but about the year 1550 Colombo became a walled city, reaching from Galle Buck on the sea down to Caymans Gate in the Pettah, and defended on the Eastern and Southern sides by the Colombo Lake. The Dutch captured the Portuguese Fort (or Castle) and kept the centre portion heavily fortified, while the town outside the walls was called The Pettah. There was a water gate leading to the open roadstead where ships lay to, near the shore on the North. On the South was the Galle Gate, where the road to Galle, 72 miles South, ran, much as it does to-day, close to the sea-shore. Inside the Fort were a few narrow roads along which no one was allowed *"to gallop on horseback or in chariots,"* — a rule one would wish to be applied severely to the driving of motor-cars to-day!

The circumference of the Fort in the 18th Century was rather more than a mile. In 1807, according to Cordiner, Colombo Fort had seven batteries, connected by intervening curtains, and was defended by 30 pieces of heavy cannon. To-day the Fort Ward, for Municipal purposes, extends to about 250 acres. But the claims of commerce in the 19th century finally prevailed, and in 1869 the old fortifications were dismantled. In 1871 most of the walls were demolished, and the Dutch Canal (still remembered by "Canal Row") that connected the Fort with the River Kelani was filled in. To-day only a few portions of the one-time massive fort walls are visible, inside H.M's Customs, and at the back of Queen's House near the Master-Attendant's bungalow, facing seaward. The cricket pitch in the Barracks Square used to be exceedingly fast, due to its standing on old concrete ramparts. It was not a pitch for a slow bowler, as I found when I played there in 1898.

To-day the city of Colombo covers an extent of many square miles. The origin of the name Colombo is not clear. Writing in 1681 Knox says — "On the West is the city of Colombo, so called from a tree the natives call *Ambo* (which bears the mango-fruit) growing in that place; but this never hath fruit but only leaves, which in their language is *cola,* and thence they called the tree Colambo; which the Christians in honour of Columbus turned to Colombo." Another suggestion is that the name is derived from Columba, or dove. These gentle birds are very common in Ceylon. It is worth noting that the Dutch coat-of-arms of Colombo shows a mango tree with a dove in the centre.

The earliest Englishman to land in Ceylon was Ralf Fitch, who visited Colombo in 1558. Another, Lancaster by name, landed at Galle in 1592. From 1659 to 1679 Robert Knox, a sailor, was, with many others, a prisoner of the King of Kandy. In 1792 Pybus visited Kandy as a British Envoy. The classic work of Knox on Ceylon is well worth careful study, being full of hard facts, shrewd comment, and humour. It is specially valuable as a first-hand record of the Kingdom of Kandy at the height of its prosperity and magnificence. Knox made valuable use of his enforced leisure, and verily led captivity captive.

The British conquerors of Ceylon in the military expedition of 1796 came from South India, and so the Island was at first administered from Fort St. George, Madras. But this was not found satisfactory; and in 1802 Ceylon became a Crown Colony by virtue of Article 5 of the Treaty of Amiens, whereby the Dutch Government at Batavia ceded and guaranteed the full property and sovereignty to His Britannic Majesty, of all its possessions and establishments in the Island.

The first Governor was the Honourable Frederick North, appointed in 1798. Ceylon was in effect a Crown Colony from the capitulation by the Dutch on February 15th, 1796, and as such the laws previously existing remained in force until altered by the conqueror. At once however, as ruled in the leading case of *Fabrigas* v. *Mostyn,* torture, which was commonly employed by the Dutch, was abolished. On September 23rd, 1799 His Majesty King George III issued a Proclamation dealing with the administration of justice and cognate matters. The first Charter of Justice is dated April 18th, 1801, which has been amended on several occasions since. In 1806 the Mohammedan (often called Muslim) Law applicable to Ceylon was codified and the *Thesawalamai,* or customary law of the Jaffna Tamils, was promulgated. The man who largely made these beneficial changes was Sir Alexander Johnston, who arrived in Ceylon in 1802 as Advocate-General in the King's Court. He became the first Chief Justice in the year 1811. He was also responsible for the introduction of trial by Jury, and on August 12th, 1816 he procured the abolition of slavery — an institution which had flourished previously. The name "Slave Island" still designates a part of Colombo. England followed Ceylon's example in this respect only 18 years later. Any person, further interested in these and kindred matters, will find them set forth luminously in Pereira's Institutes of The Laws of Ceylon, Volume I. The author was a good friend to me as a Junior Advocate, and a lawyer of great industry and learning. The present Supreme Court of the Island of Ceylon was created under the Charter of February 18th, 1833. I might mention that the legal profession is organised on the English system; Barristers here being called Advocates, and Solicitors termed Proctors. King's Counsel were first created in the year 1903.

III

After this brief retrospect of Colombo in the past, let us explore Colombo of to-day, particularly the Fort and parts adjacent thereunto, after you have booked your rooms in one of the three hotels already mentioned.

First let us enter the old Fort Church, situated just to the West of the Grand Oriental Hotel. Originally this was the main part of the official residence of the Dutch Governors. In those days, of course, Colombo was literally a Fort, with high ramparts all round, and well-guarded portcullised gates. At one time, shortly after the British occupation in 1796, this building was used for three public purposes, judicial, social, and religious. For, by day it was used as the Supreme Court; by night as a temporary theatre or ball-room; and on Sundays for Divine Service, as regulated by the Church of England. The Church was consecrated in 1821; and since then has served as the Parish Church of Colombo and provided a House of God for the Christian troops stationed in Colombo. It has some pleasant monuments to eminent Ceylonians, and the service of silver-gilt plate on the altar was a gift from King George IV, and is worth inspection.

Strolling towards the Gordon Gardens close by, we see the great stone set up by the Portuguese, mentioned later, with the national arms engraved upon it. The large white building opposite the General Post Office is Queen's House, a rambling yet charming white two-storied mansion in the Colonial style of the 18th Century. Prior to its acquisition by the British Government on January 17th, 1804, it belonged to Gerard von Angelbeek, the last Dutch Governor. His Excellency had a prodigal son-in-law employed in the Dutch Treasury. Apparently this young man helped himself liberally to public funds and owed the Treasury a large sum. His father-in-law transferred the mansion to the British Government in settlement of what was politely called this "debt." Queen's House has a charming garden on the West towards the sea, a beautiful ball-room, and an interesting portrait gallery of our past Governors. All mile-stones in Ceylon are measured to, or from, Queen's House.

The first Dutch Church built in Colombo stood where to-day stands the statue of Queen Victoria. The ground around it was the graveyard. The Dutch Supreme Court faced that church.

Until 1804 it would seem that on the site in the Fort, now occupied by Messrs. Cargills' handsome premises, originally there stood a block of old Dutch buildings, occupied by high officials, dating from 1681 when the Commandeur of Colombo lived there. Cordiner, writing in 1807, tells us that the first house which was occupied by the Hon. Frederick North on his arrival as the first Governor of Ceylon was a house in the Fort belonging to a Dutchman named Sluyskens. It would appear that Sluyskens' house was on the corner of this block. When I first came to Ceylon, Cargills' business was still carried on in the old Dutch buildings with a curious wooden statue set high up in the gable, as shown in the delightful sketch. The statue, carved in some hard wood, probably represents Minerva, the Roman Goddess of War. I imagine that some Dutch official obtained it, possibly from a Dutch man-o-war, and set it up as the palladium on which the safety of Colombo depended. This interesting relic can still be seen, carefully preserved, in Messrs. Cargills' ground floor. So it seems clear that this old Dutch House was the first "King's House" in Ceylon. The date on the foundation-stone is 1684. Captain Sluyskens was a genial soul, who had a Kaffir Band that played sweet music on the lawn in front of his house. Captain Sluyskens was wealthy, and much liked by the British Officers, whom he entertained freely. He thus promoted good feeling between Dutch and British, and it is worth noting that ever since both Dutch and British have been on terms of friendship.

Galle Face, so-called, was originally the *glacis* levelled by the military authorities, so that the guns of the Fort could sweep the open ground to the South in case of attack. Incidentally, owing to its strategic importance Galle Face has always been, and still is, military land. Galle Face originally was unpleasant by reason of the red dust that was blown about by sea-breezes from the cabook soil. Accordingly the then Governor, Sir Henry Ward, in 1853 constructed a nice walk *"for the sake of the ladies and children of Colombo in whose interest he recommended it to the care of his successors."* Galle Face soon became the favourite resort of the inhabitants of Colombo — and still is. The Noah's Ark-like building near the War Memorial is the Colombo Club, which was originally used as the grand-stand when horse-racing took place in Colombo on Galle Face. In the late 'seventies I can dimly recall seeing, as a small boy, a horse fall and break his fetlock near the old cemetery. Military bands used to play here regularly of an evening, and the wealth, rank, and beauty of Ceylon foregathered for the exchange of courtesies, compliments, and scandal. One famous episode occurred here, when a sporting planter turned up with coach and a four-in-hand, complete to the last detail. A local wag, in opposition, turned up next day with a peculiar local vehicle drawn by six capering bullocks!

The Council of State, situated to the North of Galle Face, faces the sea, with an immense Secretariat behind it. The tiny office of the Boy Scouts Association of Ceylon, almost washed by the waves, faces it. If the Council of State is actually sitting, an application by a visitor to the Speaker will meet with courteous reception, and secure a seat in the Speaker's Gallery, situated over the clock. From such a position an excellent opportunity is provided of seeing and hearing all that goes on in our Ceylon Parliament.

Turning back from Galle Face to the North we pass the Echelon Barracks. Close to these airy quarters in Queen Street stands an old building (long occupied by the firm of Darley, Butler) in a portion of which the last King of Kandy, after deposition, on January 24th, 1816, was confined, prior to his being deported to the Fort of Vellore in the Madras Presidency. His throne and the Kandyan regalia are shown to great advantage in the Museum in Cinnamon Gardens, having been restored recently to Ceylon from Windsor Castle by order of His late Majesty King George V. These royal relics are worthy of close and careful scrutiny.

Such is a short summary of certain features of interest in our Capital. We of Colombo certainly are dwellers in no mean city.

CHAPTER III

COLOMBO IN HISTORY

COLOMBO, the present Capital of Ceylon, is ordinarily situated on the Kelani River, and in flood times partly under it. This river rises near Adam's Peak, is 90 miles long, and is wholly free of alligators. Many other rivers are not. The city of Colombo has a population of rather less than 300,000.

The Portuguese navigators of the sixteenth century had a pleasing way of setting up a landmark in perpetual token of places they had graced with their adventurous presence. The coast of Africa is dotted with these sermons in stone. And naturally in Colombo they carved upon a rock a record of their landing in Ceylon. The rock in question, (as already mentioned) is in the Gordon Gardens, next to Queen's House, the official residence of His Excellency the Governor. It is worth a visit. The date is 1561.

The Dutch were a stout, deeply, if somewhat dourly, religious race, with a distinct gift for church-building, in which nobody in the congregation could escape the all-seeing eye of the minister. They also built solid houses very much like those in Cape Colony, with a *stoep,* and deep verandahs. Most of the Dutch houses are now modernised or destroyed. But round Galle and in parts of Colombo and far-distant Jaffna many still solidly remain, with the shell emblem carved on lintel or on door, as at the Dutch Church in Galle. And in Colombo there still stands an almost perfect Dutch House. Some years ago it was lovingly furnished by an artistic tenant in the Dutch style: and very charming it was. It still has the little winding-staircase and all the characteristics of Dutch Colonial domestic architecture. Its walls are so thick that the temperature inside is 5 degrees cooler than in other houses. (Modern builders usually design concrete houses in Colombo like Dutch ovens!) Now, alas! a garage at the rear and modern villas in front conceal it sorrowfully from the public gaze, at the junction of Base Line Road and Castle Street in the salubrious suburb of Borella, some four miles out from the Fort. If you visit the fine Y.M.C.A. building in the Fort you may see set on high in the courtyard a Dutch coat-of-arms that graced the first Dutch Fort in Colombo. It was discovered recently when the foundations were being excavated. The date is about 1717, or possibly a bit earlier.

Dutch furniture and the so-called Dutch china are other and interesting survivals of those spacious days. The Dutch East India Company used the Letters V.O.C. (Vereenigde Oost-Indische Compagnie) as their official emblem. One finds it set upon their dinner plates, their gates, and public buildings.

Not much of real untouched Dutch furniture remains in the open market. Some fine, if rather solid, pieces, are treasured by private collectors and a few more are in the Colombo Museum. None the less, enterprising itinerant purveyors still tour Colombo with a bullock-cart filled with *"very good kinds of old furnitures, Master!"* The venerable Perera, so well-known in Colombo as a dealer in antiques, now retired, used to class such things under three heads — *"Full of sús-picion"* : *"Little of sús-picion"* and *"Hondai* or *good."* Most of the bits, especially the so-called Dutch chests, are made of old wood and then plentifully covered with modern brass-work copied from the old. In point of fact the Dutchman had a careful mind, and usually only put brass on a chest where it served a useful purpose. But the modern street-dealer seems to possess plenty of brass and uses it with reckless profusion. Two chests that I possess are good examples of brass in perfect use, and brazen abuse.

One of the most useful Dutch furnishings is the great study-chair, of most ample proportions, so that the worthy Burgomaster man and his expansive spouse after a full meal of rice and curry might take his or her ease without abdominal compression. A fine example used to furnish a dignified setting for the Crown Proctor in the District Court of Chilaw. I am the happy possessor of two.

Incidentally, we owe the *punkah* to the Dutch. This useful disturber of the sultry air was invented by a Dutch Governor of Chinsurah, in India, about the year 1799. In 1801 General Macdowall introduced this novelty into Ceylon, having seen it in Bengal. It was not generally popular in Ceylon, I gather, at the start. Cordiner states that in his time (1806) the Portuguese and Dutch "*bore the heat with greater patience than the British, and having been always solicitous to exclude the natural winds from their homes, they are not inclined to create an artificial breeze.*" From this time we find the expression of "talking under the punkah."

At Kantalai Rest-house I remember that on a hot evening the Rest-house keeper politely invited us to sit outside on a bench overlooking the tank. "This seat very good for the blowing!" he said smilingly. It was. We lingered late, "Eating the air," in Eastern phraseology.

Of the so-called Dutch china (that is china made in China for the Dutch) I speak with the reserve of the non-expert but most enthusiastic collector. A few good pieces are on view in the Colombo Museum. Much of it is in the familiar blue and white; some of it is in the three-colour mode. It is not expensive and lights up a room wonderfully. There is now no antique shop in Colombo Fort; but china can still be picked up in Fort shops, and is sold by several recognised dealers. While curious folk, who grow curiouser and curiouser with every visit, hawk old plates and furniture from door to door in spite of many rebuffs. I have picked up pieces all over Ceylon, usually paying a few rupees for each. For one lovely three-colour plate, carp swimming in a pool, I paid Rs. 90. I have not yet been able to find out exactly to what period of pottery it belongs. Bargains can still be had. I got one yesterday!

But the greatest relic of Dutch Days is our Common-Law, commonly known as the Roman-Dutch Law. That it is written in a language which few Ceylon lawyers can read fluently — or, indeed, at all — is of course all in its favour. For to a layman it is thus a kind of *mumbo jumbo,* hidden away in dusty tomes elaborated by learned jurist fossils with such names as Johannes Voet, Perezius, Carpzovius, Groenewegen, van Leeuwen, and Bynkershoek. It has been attacked by some Chief Justices, and defended and rejuvenated by others, according to their knowledge or ignorance of the Latin tongue! It has been tortured into strange forms to suit modern tendencies, as in the case of libel and slander. Even so it has many excellent, if peculiar, features. What, for example, could be more admirable than that the Roman-Dutch commentators should discuss under what circumstances literary persons can obtain an order of ejectment against their neighbours who follow noisy occupations? And again, Voet in Lib, XIX. Tit, 2, lays down that among other just causes for a tenant quitting may be included the case of spectres haunting houses. But he cautiously adds, *"Such demoniacal illusions must be proved by manifest evidence, as to which much must be left to the discretion of the judge!"*

Who would not be a judge in Ceylon? Which reminds me that a visit to the Law Courts at Hultsdorf is always an enjoyable experience — except for the actual litigant. While the Colombo Police Court just across the road provides an alternative feast of tragedy and comedy.

Some people say that the Roman-Dutch Law is dying out. I doubt it: for its roots are now deep down in our legal soil, and taken all round it is a practical set of sensible rules for life and conduct as viewed through judicial spectacles in a temperature of 84° *plus* the burden of wig and robe. The system has its stalwart and most persistent rivals. English Law, like ivy on a ruined tower, is ceaselessly at work. Still the Roman-Dutch Law has survived, is surviving, and will survive, though some would wish to see it abolished entirely.

The unhappy judge, arriving in Ceylon from another colony, has other systems to expound. There is the *Thesawalamai* or customary Law of the inhabitants of Jaffna; the *Mukkuva* Law in the Eastern Province; the *Hindu* law, invoked by Tamils mainly in matters of religion; the *Mohammedan* Law and the *Kandyan* Law. In fact a choice of evils! The last-named system by the way, among other unusual features, permits polyandry — that is the joint possession by one wife of two husbands; but associated marriages are the exception, not the rule. The reason originally was economic — the labour of one man was insufficient to maintain a wife and children.

Lastly there is a mass of case law, in which the above systems have been joyfully and gloriously blended, to the great advantage of the legal profession. Out of the 37 unofficial Members of the late Legislative Council about 27 were lawyers! In the State Council to-day lawyers are numerous.

And so in 1796 we come to the British Era. No really good book has yet been written which deals truthfully and comprehensively with this entire period. Many people have written on short periods. Mr. L. J. B. Turner's book "*Collected Papers on the History of the Maritime Provinces of Ceylon* 1795-1805" is excellent. Personally I found the Cleghorn Papers most interesting. For this far-seeing Scotchman planned a means whereby Ceylon should become a British possession. He arranged with the British Government to purchase the services of Colonel de Meuron's Swiss Regiment, then forming an important part of the Dutch Garrison in Colombo. After an incredibly arduous journey Cleghorn reached Madras, and then visited the British Army besieging Colombo. He cleverly conveyed (in a Dutch cheese!) the order from Col. de Meuron to the Officer in command of his Regiment. The order was loyally obeyed, and Colombo fell.

The book by Sir J. Emerson Tennent, Colonial Secretary of Ceylon in the 'sixties, is best known. But Ceylon has changed vastly since then. Even thirty years ago things — and people — moved slowly. I have painful recollections of a trip to Batticaloa in 1899. I left Bandarawela, the then Up-country railhead, about mid-day in a so-called horse-coach. The vehicle was a ramshackle waggonette, with a tin of water suspended above each of the wooden brakes to keep them from bursting into flame on the long downhill run. The horses were not real horses: for usually two of them only possessed five sound legs all-told. Badulla was reached for lunch, and thence we painfully climbed up to Passara and, more by the grace of God than anything else, reached Lunugalla for dinner — about 45 weary miles from the start. After the meal a lumbering bullock-cart arrived at the Rest-house for any unhappy passengers. The vehicle in question bore the alluring title

"ROYAL MAIL"

The mails came first, ladies (if any) came second, and we were a very poor third. All night we jogged on through the jungle and at dawn had a hasty early tea at a jungle Rest-house. About midnight, or even later, after some twenty-eight hours' continuous bumpy motion we — or rather what was left of us — arrived at Batticaloa.

In those days budding lawyers certainly earned their fees when they were briefed to appear in distant outstations.

The car and the advent of electric light and electric fans have certainly enormously improved conditions of living in Ceylon.

The bicycle also has many uses. The first time a cyclist passed a certain house in Colombo the *ayah* was in the garden. *"Look, lady look"* she cried out to her mistress, excitedly, *"One master sitting and going!"*

This unsymmetrical chronicle is not greatly concerned with the obvious sights of Colombo — such as its Museum, its snake-charmers, and its public buildings — all of which require little commentary here. Be it remembered, however, that the Y.M.C.A. in the Fort is a fine building, excellently managed, with good food at most reasonable rates. A younger sister, the Y.W.C.A. in Union Place, is worth a visit too. And at the Headquarters of the Boy Scouts Association of Ceylon on Galle Face opposite the State Council, every Boy Scout of every race will be welcomed and helped in every way. The Girl Guides too flourish in Ceylon, having charming Headquarters in the Cinnamon Gardens, at the Turret Road end of Edinburgh Crescent. The splendid Soldiers' and Sailors' Institute in the same block as the Y.M.C.A. offers everything that the most exacting soldier or sailor could wish for. Airmen simply fly to it.

Here perhaps I may say a word about shopping in Colombo — the beloved pursuit of every true woman. It may be noted here that when you land at the jetty you are (to use a Sinhalese expression) "within a loud hoo-cry" of every commodity you can possibly require. In England we should say, "within a stone's throw," I suppose. As regards big stores you have a wide choice, with Cargills and Millers; who also have branches Up-country: not to mention many smaller concerns. For Oriental goods there are many good shops, mostly in Chatham Street, where silks and stuffs of the East are brilliantly exposed. Near the Clock Tower are the fine premises of the Ceylon Cottage Industries Depôt. Here is a wide range of Ceylon handcrafts of the highest class of local workmanship, and you can buy many charming and useful articles that make such nice gifts to friends at home, in the Dominions, or abroad. Many of these gifts are quite inexpensive — such as the hats and baskets from Kalutara. If you collect baby elephants, you will find them here by hundreds. All prices are fixed, and you have the satisfaction of knowing that the village-worker has been paid a fair wage. In Ceylon there is too much sweated labour, with the inevitable result. The Cottage Industries Shop, and the Marketing Board see that a fair wage is earned, and paid. If you wish to buy tea to take away, you can get it from The Westown Tea Co., at Hirdaramani's shop in Chatham Street. It is packed in air-tight packets and will be delivered to you on board your ship.

I might mention here that if you wish to take motion-pictures in colour of scenes in Colombo, you will find that the morning and late afternoon is better than the blazing sunshine of mid-day. Cloudy days, too, give excellent results with an absence of deep shadows.. An exposure-meter, I find (though I have been taking photographs for 40 years) is essential for perfect results.

But there are many people who wish to see a bit of the East, to get some of the real Oriental atmosphere. For that one must go to the Pettah, which is the Ceylonese trade-centre of Ceylon, and as busy as any nest of industrious ants. Here many peoples are represented — Sinhalese, Tamils; Moormen, (as Ceylon Muslims are often called) Parsees, Afghans (really Pathans) Chetties — and many more. Here too congregate motor-buses from every part of the Island. Muslim houses are easily noted;

Close latticed to the brooding heat.

For although the younger generation is in favour of relaxation of *purdah* (literally, 'curtain'), most Muslim ladies still live very retired lives.

Here, too, you can gaze on
The busy Town's tumultuous crowds.

Tinkling trams, bullock-carts, buses, cars, and rickshaws jostle pedestrians, who always prefer the roadway to the pavement. It is a jolly scene — one that I never tire of watching.

The best way is to take a car or a rickshaw, and go down Main Street. Get out at one of the many Indian shops where they sell silks and *sarees.* These things range in price from two pounds up to a hundred or more, and are really very beautiful.

And when the shop-keeper with reckless profusion strews the counter with endless pieces, the feast of flaming colour is extraordinarily fascinating. Here too are silver and gold tissues at prices which are very low. Ask to be shown the work-rooms: and you will see small boys and be-spectacled old men working by hand and patterning the gleaming silk with every sort of design at a truly remarkable rate of speed.

And then go to the Municipal Vegetable and Fruit Market at the back of the old Town Hall. The best time of day is early in the morning: but the Market is open all day. Here, in season, you can get papoys, mangosteens, mangoes, plantains, pine-apples, *kurumbas,* avocado pears, and every kind of weird-looking vegetable, whose merits are vociferously proclaimed in surroundings beside which Babel was a dome of silence and Covent Garden a place of rest. And after that go slowly down Sea Street, the Lombard Street of Colombo, where the money-lenders, called Chetties, from Southern India mostly congregate. Great wealth exists in this quiet street, with the *vilasam* or firm-name painted over the door. The Chetties live largely on milk, and *Ghee* which gives them a sleek and comfortable appearance. Inside each house lives a large cow, as sleek as her proprietor. Ghee, which is simply butter boiled to make it keep, denotes richness and well-being. It has an infallible effect on the Chetty's figure. Of such a man the Indian proverb says — *"He has five fingers in the Ghee pot."* Frugal people only insert two. The Chetty also uses *Ghee* as a lubricant for the skin after bathing. You will remember how in the Old Testament butter was an emblem of luxury. In the Song of Deborah is written :—

He asked water, and she gave him milk:
She brought him butter in a lordly dish.

Once long ago I paid a visit with two English ladies to a certain Chetty's boutique in Sea Street. In those days all Chetties kept *ola* books of account — that is a file of palm leaves covered with writing. The method of writing is interesting. The *Kannickapulli* (or clerk) grows his left thumb-nail to an immense length. At the tip he cuts a V-shaped nick. He then puts the palm-leaf in his left hand, thumb facing upwards. He picks up with his right hand a sharp-pointed instrument, and fits it into the nick on his nail. Then as he passes the palm-leaf towards the left he scratches words and figures on it with incredible speed and accuracy. When the scratching is finished he smears ink over it. The scratched portion comes out dark and the rest of the ink is wiped off the non-absorbent part of the palm-leaf. This performance is most fascinating. At the Temple of the Tooth in Kandy, the Librarian, who is a learned Buddhist Priest, will gladly display his graphic merits as a stylist on palm-leaf.

On the occasion in question the polite Chetty whom we visited presented each lady with an *ola* on which the K. P. had written this pleasing composition :—

> *"The Dorai came with two ladies to the boutique.*
>
> *They saw the Chetty.*
>
> *They saw the Cow*
>
> *And were much pleased."*

But Sea Street is at its best about dusk. Pass down it slowly at that grey hour and peep through richly-carved doorways into the Hindu Temples, where the white-robed Chetties are silhouetted against the great idol set in its frame of twinkling lights, while the tom-tom and the shrill pipe summon the worshippers to prayer in a heavy atmosphere of scented chaplets of white and yellow flowers.

That is the real East. And in that street you will see represented all the diverse peoples of Southern India and Ceylon.

Close by stands Wolfendhal Church. In the Pettah still stands The Belfry that summoned the Dutch to Church at Kaymans Gate. ('Kaymans' means crocodiles; who lay close by in the lake, which washed in those days the edge of Main Street). The date over the entrance is 1749. The letters

J.V.S.V.G.

are the initials of the Dutch Governor, van Gollenesse, who rose from the rank of

Serjeant	...	1723
Lieutenant	...	1729
Kapitin	...	1730
Commander of Malabar	...	1733

to be Governor of Ceylon 1743, and finally went to Batavia in the capacity of Director-General of the Dutch East Indies.

The great door of Wolfendhal Church is often closed, but there is a school attached to the Church at the back, and the Church *appu* on application can generally obtain the keys. On Sunday divine worship takes place according to the forms of the Dutch Reformed Church.

On entering one is attracted by the font, which is a fine piece of carving set on three massive legs. A silver basin fits into the top. The basin two feet in diameter and weighing 206¾ rupees, was presented to the Church by Rycloff van Goens and his wife in memory of their daughter Esther Ceylonia, who was the first child to be baptised out of it on June 17th, 1668.

The name Ceylonia is attractive. Other local geographical names suitable for female infants are Diyatalawa and Urugasmanhandiya, which may be used without a fee or charge of any kind. The daughter of a recent Governor revived this charming fashion by taking the name Neliya — a shortened form of Nuwara Eliya, where she was born. The place in question is locally pronounced "Newraliya."

The organ is small, but capable of much harmony; as proved by Herr Hellmann, a gifted musician from Vienna, who (by permission) played to us one afternoon.

The pulpit at Wolfendahl is a stately edifice with a charming stair and hand-rail. Opposite the pulpit is the great box-pew that was occupied by the Dutch Governor, while other, though less stately enclosures, were reserved for high officials. Some interesting tomb-stones and mural memorials give us peeps into the lives and deaths of the great men of the period. On the night of September 4th, 1813, the remains of five Dutch Governors, and their families, some 25 in all, were removed from the old graveyard to Wolfendahl in full ceremony, the British Governor attending in State. I like best of all, perhaps, the old chairs of delicate 18th Century work, of which about 50 still remain, carved with the emblem of the period and made of calamander, ebony, and nedun.

Not so far from Wolfendahl is the Boy Scout Training Camp at Mutwal, beautifully situated at the root of the northern arm of the breakwater. All those interested in the Boy Scout

Movement are made welcome here. But it is as well, perhaps, to visit the office of the Boy Scouts Association of Ceylon first and arrange a visit with the Secretary.

Just before reaching the Camp you will pass the picturesque harbour where the Colombo fishing fleet lies. Scores of sea-going *catamarans* are beached here, and you may for a few shillings go for a short sail on one of these engaging craft under

The dark-brown sheet of the fishing-canoe,
As she skims the waters of foam-tipped blue.

These clumsy yet engaging craft are similar to those mentioned by Strabo, Pliny, and Solinus, as being used during their time in Eastern Waters, and are therefore some of the oldest craft in the world.

An Englishman loves his Club. And it is worth noting that the first English Club in Ceylon, appropriately named *"The Cocoa Nut,"* was founded in Mutwal about 1800 at a house later known as "Whist Bungalow" overlooking the mouth of the Kelani River. At this time the English circle in Colombo consisted of "about one hundred gentlemen and only twenty ladies."

They were thrilling times for women! No wonder we read that one lady had wedded and buried two husbands before she was nineteen!

If you like what Soames Forsyte called "Bigotry and Virtue," visit the Auction Rooms in Baillie Street, and meet Col. J. G. Vandersmagt, who will show you, perhaps, a nice bit of old silver, porcelain, or some other delightful possession sent to him for disposal. In these rooms I have acquired several treasures, rich and rare, at most reasonable prices. Again at Mr. H. M. Gunasekera's Rooms at 87, Union Place, Slave Island, you may find a bargain. It was there that I bought my excellent copy of Knox's Ceylon dated 1681, in almost perfect condition out of the Chillingworth Castle Library.

At "Arts and Crafts," near the P. & O. office, I have bought many charming Ceylon articles that make delightful gifts. They are sold at reasonable prices, and are of good quality.

And now from these varied surroundings we return to our modern hotel for a bath and dinner, bringing one clear impression home — that Colombo on the whole is the cleanest Capital in the East.

CHAPTER IV

THE SOUTHERN PROVINCE

NOW it is time to look further afield, where fresh woods and pastures green await you, in varying degrees and shades of loveliness. I propose to take you on a series of quiet tours, such as I have often done leisurely myself. You can see the outline of this Land of Promise clearly, if you lift up your eyes Eastwards from Colombo early in the morning, before the mist has blotted out the many ranges of blue hills, with Adam's Peak proudly rearing its sacred head above all others. 'Hasten slowly' is the golden rule of travel, especially in Ceylon.

Ordinarily you go, in these days, by train (that is by the Ceylon Government Railway) or by car.

For a comparatively small Island it is remarkable that such an extensive system of rail-roads exists in almost every part of the country.

Lately I travelled down by the morning train from Kandy to Colombo and, (though I have so often seen it all before) took in deep breaths of clean air and re-charged my spirit with great vistas of rural beauty. Rarely, I imagine, does a traveller get a better visual cross-section of any country than the train gives on this 70-mile run. The Ceylon Government Railway goes almost all over Ceylon : fares are cheap : and season tickets for travel-as-you-please are available at Rs. 50 for a fortnight, and Rs. 75 for a month. Cheap week-end tickets to Nuwara Eliya enable one to leave Colombo on Friday night at 9-40 p.m. and reach Nuwara Eliya in time to start golf or fishing by 8 next morning. One leaves again on Sunday night, to arrive in Colombo about 7-30 a.m. in great form for another week's work. The journey up from Kandy to Badulla gives one a cross-section of Up-country, where tea-carpets cover the hill-sides with masses of virgin jungle as background. For a large party a delightful special saloon — a Club on wheels — is available at little extra cost. There is a refreshment-car on most important trains, and to engineers this broad-gauge line carried up to over 6,000 feet past formidable obstacles presents features of much technical interest. The above fares are first-class.

Recently the Railway has imported three beautiful Diesel Trains, called Silver Foam, Silver Spray, and Silver Mist. Two of these trains run regularly to Galle in just over two hours. Another train runs to Matara, further on, passing Weligama, beloved of bathers. Travelling in these trains is definitely delightful, and I strongly advise all tourists to use them.

If you go by car you have, of course, more freedom, and will find Ceylon roads — once called "The Best in the World" — very good on the whole.

As to cars, I would suggest that to ensure satisfaction you should go to one of the several reputable firms who can be relied on. Cars of every kind, including (till lately) weird relics of Mr. Henry Ford's early days, are obtainable. But I advise you to avoid them.

Not long ago a lady who hired a cheap motor vehicle heard a tinkling unusual sound. Then the car stopped.

"What's the matter?" she asked.

"I think carburetter falling out," said the smiling driver.

"Well, ask it to fall in again!" she said tartly.

Which it did, quite cheerfully — being tied up with a bit of coir-rope. And on they went till it fell out again!

In early days of motoring in Ceylon I had many dilatory and painful experiences, including an occasion when a two-ton Wolseley phaeton turned upside down on top of four of us — without causing damage to passengers or vehicle. In these days cars, of course, are far more reliable, and petrol and accessories are available everywhere. Personally I know, and can therefore recommend, the fine fleet of cars maintained by Armstrong's Tourist Agency, with an office (facing the jetty) at 14, York Arcade. The drivers are reliable — an important point. If you are making a longer stay, it might possibly pay you to buy a good second-hand car from Rowlands Garages. They have a big department for used cars of every kind, and guarantee to re-purchase a car at a fixed price. Their spacious premises are in Turret Road, in the Cinnamon Gardens, two miles from the Fort.

If you drive yourself, remember that buffaloes and pedestrians usually claim the middle of the road by prescription.

There are various excellent Tourist Agencies in Colombo, where you can get expert advice on trips and tours, and correct information on every matter. As their name is legion, I will not offer advice as to choice. Most travellers are already booked, and well served from the start. As regards guides, I personally would avoid them in Colombo, for they are really unnecessary. All persons touting should be coldly repulsed : if they are persistent, ask a policeman's aid. The effect is magical. In the Buried Cities the guides are fairly well informed, and are worth while engaging. The first guide at Polonnaruwa is the best of all

If you are going to tour mainly for sport, it is a case of Arms for the Man and Clothes for the Woman — each out to conquer the jungle. Most people, however, now wear shirts and shorts, so I need not say any more on costume. As I am not an authority on big-game shooting, I will just refer visiting sportsmen to the courteous officials of the Ceylon Game Protection Society. The Honorary Secretary may be addressed "c/o The Mercantile Bank, Colombo."

Here I would mention three valuable reference works of real merit in Ceylon : (1) *Ferguson's Directory*, published by *The Ceylon Observer.* (2) *The Green Book*, published by *The Times of Ceylon*, and (3) *The Hand-book*, issued by the Automobile Association of Ceylon. Many people on arrival say, "I used to know a fellow called Smith." Anyone's address can be found in the above publications, and friends are always worth looking up. The Government Tourist Bureau, with a representative Committee, is always ready to give travellers valuable advice and help.

An admirable suggestion has been made that this office, (with others like the Tea Propaganda Board), should be housed in new buildings on either side of the approach-road to the Jetty. Then every traveller on landing, would see an epitome of All Ceylon and could get every possible help and information at one centre.

The writer of Proverbs reminds us that there is a time for everything under the sun. Take heed to his words, for many inexperienced travellers pursue English hours in the East with an orthodox hour for breakfast and lunch : but that means you miss much. The time to see wild Ceylon is from just before dawn to ten o'clock. Then rest, and have a late breakfast. Start again about four o'clock and motor as much as possible in the late afternoon and evening. For otherwise, especially along the jungle-roads, you will see little of bird or beast in the heat of the day. The butterflies, however, are in evidence all day long, and very lovely they are, especially in the Eastern Province. If these lovely painted ladies of the jungle appeal to you, go straight to Messrs. Cave & Co.'s Book Department in Colombo and buy a copy of *"The Butterflies of Ceylon"* by the late Mr. W. Ormiston.

As regards birds, you can buy *Familiar Birds of Ceylon,* illustrated, by Cicely Kershaw, or *Birds of Ceylon* by W. E. Wait. If you want coloured plates, the work of G. M. Henry is amazingly good. It is rather fun to try and compile a list, as you tour, of all the birds you see and can name by reference to one of these books.

If you take my advice, you will live a simple open-air existence, as far as possible. The golden rule is to take as little luggage as possible: for she that increaseth baggage increaseth sorrow. If you are going actually to camp out, study the chapter on camping in Dr. Spittel's *"Wild Ceylon,"* where he gives minute details, acquired by long experience. For ordinary touring purposes a simple outfit will suffice.

In the big stores in Colombo, like Cargills' and Miller's, you can get all that is needful. They also have branches Up-country in Kandy and Nuwara Eliya. In the olden days one took ample stores on tour. To-day that is unnecessary. But personally I always take Bovril, chocolate, and biscuits. Then in the rare event of an involuntary stop, you can have a good meal. I venture to suggest (on the advice of my wife) that you take a little linen with you on a long tour — your own soft pillow, and two light cotton sheets. They are rather nice in some Rest-houses after a long and tiring day, and sometimes may add freshness to a Rest-house bed. I might here mention Mr. H. W. Cave's immortal comment on Rest-house furniture long ago. He showed a picture of a most dilapidated long-chair in a verandah. Underneath he wrote —

"A rush-bottomed chair with the bottom rushed out."

"Mosquitoline," Flit, or something similar, is useful to keep off stinging insects of every kind. If bitten, ammonia and water will allay your irritation. Here I will quote from the *Jungle Tide* by John Still — to which great book I refer later in detail.

"When Burton wandered in Somaliland in the eighteen fifties the natives, he said, did not permit strangers to interfere with the bats that haunted their huts, for these were supposed to live upon mosquitoes, whose bite *'they erroneously believed'* to be the cause of fever! Have the Veddahs some ancient memory of a Charles Darwin, and the Somalis of a prehistoric Ronald Ross?"

As regards food on tour, eggs and poultry are usually plentiful and the Rest-house Keeper will roast a bird to take along in the car with you. If you have a gun (and a licence) you can add game in season — snipe, golden-plover, jungle-fowl, or many kinds of brightly-plumaged pigeons. Have them roasted with a little curry sauce and eat them cold, if you want to taste the food of the jungle gods. While Up-country between May and October your rod can give you many a nice half-pound trout to grill in butter — lots of butter, please. The Honorary Secretary of the Ceylon Fishing Club, Nuwara Eliya, will give you particulars and issue a licence, by the day, week or month. In Nuwara Eliya the trout-stream is at your door. It contains literally thousands of good fish that come up from Lake Gregory.

As regards the Low-country, below say 1,500 feet, the climate is warm. Above 1,500 feet beware of chills, as the temperature drops rapidly about an hour before sunset. I always slip on something warm and woolly about 5-30, or even earlier. With these preliminary observations we are now ready to start on our trip through Ceylon. Here, the golden rule is *"start early."* Nature has been defined as the only thing feminine that never speaks. But that is a libel. Nature is a true woman with a great gift of speech, and nature never speaks so movingly as at dawn, when every bird takes up the full-throated hymn of praise. Personally I go to bed very early in the jungle, and am out and about before daylight; so that I can watch the Chariot of Dawn, drawn by seven Yellow Horses, rise up gloriously in the East.

Let us go South for our first expedition. We will leave Colombo very early, before anybody is up and about, and reach Ambalangoda early, about 54 miles along the coast, and bathe in the lovely rock-bound sea-pool, perpetually fed with hissing waves. If, however, you are interested in Boy Scouts, on the way you should turn off at the 27th mile on crossing the big bridge over the Kalu-Ganga, just as you enter the pretty town of Kalutara South. Part of the old Fort is still showing on the hill here, and scout-signs will direct you to the Scout Colony, some three miles away on your left. This is a Back-to-the-land Settlement, run generally on Scout lines by the Chief Commissioner of Scouts, and exceedingly well-organised. Here Scouts after a thorough course of training, are fitted to go out and open up forest land for themselves. The resident staff will give you a warm welcome. Visitors from all over the world have learned much from this bold yet severely practical experiment. The Colony has very lovely surroundings.

At the 38th milestone you will pass Bentota Rest-house, famous for its lighthouse and fresh oysters. It used to be said that at night the oysters came ashore and roosted in the trees. This was told once to a young Scottish banker, who had just arrived in Ceylon at Galle, and was on his way to Colombo. "In Aberdeen," he replied, "we juist ca' them 'Branch Banks !'"

After breakfast — an excellent meal can always be had at Bentota or Ambalangoda Rest-houses — we motor on to Galle, with entrancing glimpses of the foaming sea breaking over golden sands that are studded with coconut trees.

At the end of a gorgeous run of 72 miles you will see the huge Galle Fort rising up out of the sea, with frowning ramparts pierced by two great portcullised gates. On the inner aspect of the harbour gate is inscribed

ANNO MDCLXIX.

This gate is worthy of careful notice, for it proudly displays the Dutch arms, with the cock above, and the V.O.C. inset, in the centre beneath the shell. The Fort is in almost perfect condition and on a dark night one can still see in fancy the stalwart sentries keeping watch. Many a bloody battle has raged round these walls, and around the older fort that existed previously.

Captain Sluyskens' House.

Knox's Ceylon.

Execution by an Elephant.

to send one. The Master of the British ship promptly fired a round shot, which crashed through the dining-room where the Dutch Governor was having his dinner.

He got his pilot.

One thinks of another Dutch Governor, Petrus Vuyst. At the age of 30 he arrived at Galle, and on landing his first act was to clap a plaster over one eye; just to show that he did not require two eyes to rule so small a country. He was a most unpleasant fellow: among other vile practices he used to have his victim's nails pulled out and hot sealing-wax dropped on the bleeding flesh. But he got his deserts; he was tried for his atrocities and found guilty at Batavia. He was first decapitated, then quartered, then burned, and finally his ashes flung into the sea. On the other hand many of the Dutch Governors were wise and good administrators, God-fearing men of high principle and great ability.

The Galle ramparts in the moonlight with the Southern Cross blazing across the sparkling sea provide a walk to be remembered.

If you prefer to go to Galle by train, you will have a very lovely journey, that now takes only 2 hours or so by a fast train. After dinner, (or early next morning) we move on in fairy-like surroundings to Weligama — a jolly little Dutch Rest-house by the sea. The oysters here are excellent and the sea-bathing superb. Both are quite safe. Incidentally be it noted that sea-bathing in Ceylon is sometimes dangerous owing to currents, but there is no fear of sharks close into shore. Weligama affords good sea-fishing too from a *catamaran*. The Rest-house Keeper, as many another, can put up an excellent chicken-fish-egg-and-vegetable-curry with samballs, the very remembrance of which brings tears of flavour to your eyes.

Just near the level-crossing at Weligama you pass by the so-called Custa-Raja — a great stone figure of a Sinhalese King who was miraculously cured here of a painful complaint. I love Weligama; and hope some day to try the sea-fishing, which is, by repute, first-class.

A few more words about Rest-house food may be useful. Fish, of course, is always excellent by the sea. But you should send a post-card giving the Rest-house Keeper fair notice. Even in the jungle excellent *Lulu* fish are procurable from the tanks The man at Sigiri keeps a few in a tub, ready for the pan. At Polonnaruwa, once long ago, the Boy told us he *shot* the fish for dinner. As we looked incredulous he explained in his limited English, "That quite true, Lady, I not telling Master and Lady any lies. First I am keeping some pig-meat long time till *ishtinking* very nicely. Then Punch-appu — that our house-cooly, Lady — putting meat on a long pole in the water. Then plenty fish running to bite the *ishmell* — then —" a dramatic pause to take aim — "I shoot, Lady!" And it was all quite true.

It has often occurred to me that a very original and almost unexplored fund of curious wit is to be found in the world of Rest-house Keepers. They are of every kind. Their king was Tamby, now with God, who reigned in Trincomalee for half-a-century and was the friend of the Royal Navy. Two more stories close our chestnuts.

"Anybody staying in the Rest-house, Boy?" asked a visitor. "One gentleman and two Planters, Master!" said the Boy politely.

And when asked recently what could be had for early tea the Boy replied, "Cannot give much these days, Master. Only a good kind of bacon and some little big eggs."

Some day perhaps a monograph will be written giving these worthy fellows and their quaintly-worded bills a fitting place in literature. "Sickin minsh" is a very good dish.

Rest-houses in Ceylon vary according to time, place, quantity, quality, and the mood of the Rest-house Keeper. Negombo has a huge pile; in the jungle it may be just a mud-hut. I personally rather prefer the latter, the *pukka* Rest-house in the jungle. Close to the road these places stand, fragile erections of mud, daubed yellow outside, white-washed within, and with a tarred line at the base to ward off white-ants. The roof of cadjan is low, held up by jungle-sticks, and the floor of cement or just plain earth. All are fully furnished.

The plan is simple. In front is a verandah. Then comes an open hall, where meals are served. Out of this right and left, like some stage-plan, are bedrooms, furnished in simple fashion with wooden beds. A small inner room, like the Black Hole of Calcutta, is the bath-room — often without an actual bath. But an empty jam-tin and a bucket filled with water invite you to perform splashing ablutions of a most cooling and refreshing kind. This room, when not occupied by a guest, often serves as a quiet retreat for a sitting-hen. And thereby hangs one little tale, that I most regretfully, must omit! Many people sigh for the simple life. In such a Rest-house you get it.

Few things are more pleasant after a long day than to swing in through the gate of a Rest-house like Maha Oya in the dusk. The Boy comes out. A car is under the porch. What a nuisance — one always likes to have the whole Rest-house to one's self. But the Boy explains.

"That Master gone away, leaving car here, Sir. I think car not feeling quite well." I know that kind of car!

One clamours for immediate bibition, and sinks gratefully into a long chair. After dinner one sits outside, while ten thousand crickets praise the Creator with maddening monotony. Beyond — darkness: and from it comes the hum of the jungle, that indescribable weird, subdued, reverberation. If it has been raining during the day there is the fitful drip from the trees, while flickering fire-flies prove that love in the jungle laughs at rain. For a few yards round the building the ground is open — a little space that man has wrested from the jungle, but which the jungle is always valiantly striving to reconquer. For man in Maha Oya has enjoyed but a few years of adverse possession against the jungle's prescriptive title of a million years. Jungle never rests.

Close to Weligama Rest-House stands the little Island called 'Taprobane,' on which Count de Mauny has built a most delightful house, and made a modern Garden of Eden — without any Serpent. If you buy his book — *The Gardens of Taprobane* — at Cave's in Colombo, you will read all about this lovely Island and its many treasures; to which Nature and Art have contributed bountifully. Visitors are welcomed by the Count, who is a most delightful host.

We now pass on to Matara, situated on the Nil Ganga (Blue River) full of alligators.

The two Lawrences, so famous in Indian history, were born in Matara. Their mother used to speak of them as her "Matara Diamonds."

Matara has two Dutch forts, of which the Star Fort is highly picturesque. The Rest-house is large and comfortable. A few miles further on, keeping close to the sea, we reach Dondra Head, the last bit of land South till you meet the South Pole. Stop on the way for an hour at Dondra Village and drive down towards the lighthouse. In the rock pools and eddies here you will find lovely sea-creatures, spongy, silky, and of strange shape, with gorgeous colouring in the light of the sun. I know of no other place in Ceylon quite like this. But remember, at sunset the colours fade and the sea-world goes to bed under the dark rocks. I think that long long ago the end of a big rainbow fell into the sea off Dondra, and still goes on colouring the fish with scales of many colours. We soon go on again, and reach Tangalle after about 30 miles more, switchbacking up and down low hills, above delightful coves with great stretches of golden sands, on which the sea thunders and spumes; a Paradise for beach-lovers.

Tangalle Rest-house is beautifully situated just above the sea. Its dining-room contains the usual illustrated mosquito literature warning one against *anopheles*. On entering this room once I remarked to the Rest-house Keeper, "Plenty anopheles, I suppose, Boy?" "Are no fleas here, Sir," he replied indignantly.

Turtle are plentiful here, and are sometimes shot, as they bob up suddenly in the sea fifty yards from the Rest-house verandah. If shot dead, they are washed ashore next day. Close to the Rest-house stands a good group of ebony trees — rather a rare sight in a Ceylon town.

All along the Eastern coast the seas are really fine — great green rollers lined with silver thundering in, then breaking into snow-white surf on the yellow shore fringed with emerald-green coconuts; above, the bluest of skies. Then we go on along a switch-back road, till we enter the dry zone of Hambantota. But about the 138th mile, we turn to the left and enter the wilds. All the way up to Madampe it is jungle country and you may see anything — elephants, deer, leopards, a bear, monkeys, all the Ceylon jungle beasts one sees in the Zoo, with birds and butterflies in due season.

We once met some travellers who were full of a strange and wonderful adventure with a huge wild elephant on this road. Later we questioned the driver of the car — a puny lad of eighteen.

"What did the elephant really do to you?" we asked.

"Nothing, Master — only little blowing through the nose," he replied scornfully.

Towards evening as you approach the blue foot-hills of Sabaragamuwa you pass again into cultivated country.

If you dine on the road near Madampe you will make Ratnapura in time for bed. From there it is only 54 miles back to Colombo through endless villages, paddy-fields, and tea and rubber estates.

About twelve miles south of Ratnapura is the Sinharaja Forest, about 26 miles in length, and some 90 square miles in extent. It is south-west of Rakwana, and north-west of Deniyaya. The forest runs from 300-3,800 feet above sea level. The few inhabitants are Kandyan Sinhalese, Buddhists by religion. I quote from a most interesting article (*The Geographical Journal,* June, 1937), by Mr. John R. Baker. He writes :—

> "The Sinharaja presents the typical characters of a virgin tropical rain-forest. It is the only considerable area of such forest left in Ceylon, though formerly the whole of the low-country wet zone must have been similarly clothed. It is remarkable for the straightness of the stems of the trees, which are branched only high above the ground, and for the almost universal development of drip-points to the leaves. The climate is equable, with some rain at all seasons; but most of the trees show seasonal phenomena in reproduction, and some of the largest are deciduous. It is greatly to be hoped that the forest will be preserved in its natural state, as a record of the former condition of a large part of the Island."

In the past few people realized that a forest is an elaborate mechanism of Nature for the control and absorption of rainfall. The rich carpet of accumulated leaf-mould round the roots of forest trees acts as an absorbent sponge, which sucks in the water as it falls and then releases it gradually into the springs, which, in turn, feed the rivers. By this gradual process the rivers are kept flowing in manageable volume all the time, instead of bursting into flood at times of heavy rainfall and drying up when the rain holds off. In addition, forests help to control the incidence of rainfall. When rain-clouds during our monsoons meet the column of warm air rising from a hot bare tract of country they rise and become thinner; but when they meet the cooler air over a forest they become chilled and tend to condense and fall as rain. Thus the preservation of forests, as a natural check and balance on water supply, has an important bearing on food supply as well.

Ratnapura, by interpretation *The City of Gems*, is the capital of the Province of Sabaragamuwa, and is the centre of the gemming industry, which is carried on usually under legal licence from Government, but often illicitly. The methods are crude, the pits being excavated by hand, and bamboo poles supply any scaffolding required. Many people seek gems in the streams. Yet big valuable gems — rubies, sapphires, star-sapphires, alexandrites, and many others — are found by lucky adventurers. One thinks of the pearl-fishers of Paracelsus:

Two points in the adventure of the diver;
One — when a beggar, he prepares to plunge:
One — when a prince, he rises with his pearl.

Thus in 1907 in Kuruwita Korle, near Ratnapura, was found the glorious sapphire that weighed 466 carats after being cut. It was sold by the famous Colombo jewellers, O. L. M. Macan Markar, to the late Mr. Pierpont Morgan, of New York, a great collector. Another stone found at Pelmadulla in 1926 weighed over 400 carats after being cut and polished. The gem-cutters are usually Ceylon Moors from the village of Veenagoda near Beruwela, on the Western coast. The gem-seekers are usually Sinhalese. Moors are expert valuers, cutters, and polishers. Ceylon gems are not easy to cut, as often their colour is not constant all through the gem. In Colombo you should visit the big shop of Macan Markar in the Grand Oriental Hotel. There you will see and can handle a glorious sapphire nearly two inches long and an inch and three-quarters wide. Incidentally, you can buy it for a mere £30,000 sterling. This famous firm of Macan Markar was founded in 1860 by the late O. L. M. Macan Markar, and has a modern Aladdin's Cave that you can inspect free. Here you will see a collection of precious heirlooms of the family — pieces of old Moorish ancestral gold-jewellery, set with precious stones. It is a most fascinating display, and probably unique. I could spend hours here studying these specimens of the jeweller's art of long ago.

Star-sapphires may be had in an interesting range of colours. They vary from a pale-gray of morning light with just the merest suggestion of blue, to one of vivid midnight hue. Such depth of colour, however, is very rare; the lighter shades predominating. It is in these lighter, more hazy colours, that the star is most distinctly seen. When fortunate enough to obtain a stone of dark rich blue, (free from the imperfections found often at the back of the Star-sapphire), encasing a prominent star, you have then surely obtained a stone of miraculous blending and unsullied beauty — the pride of the Orient! Happily this matrix or carbon found on the back of the stone in no way mars its beauty or value, and often may be eliminated by careful and artistic mountings. This is, without doubt, the favourite stone of visitors to Ceylon.

There is an interesting Hindu legend about these Star-sapphires. It tells how, if you wear the stone on your left hand, it will guard you from any foreshadowing evil that might assail you. They say the star is symbolic of captive fire, worshipped for the protection of mortals. Under all symbolism lies a truth. Who can say what secret light, quiet contemplation of the Star-sapphire may not reveal!

A visit to the Museum of Ceylon precious stones formed by Mr. N. D. H. Abdul Caffoor in Church Street, next door to the G.O.H. should be included in your tour of Colombo.

Ratnapura is in the heart of the tea-cum-rubber and pure rubber industry. You can easily obtain permission to visit an estate, and learn how rubber from bark, and tea from bush, come to their destiny, as pneumatic tyre or aromatic drink. The 52-mile drive to Colombo by way of Avisawella is a very beautiful one, and you gain charming glimpses at times of Adam's Peak, which is a little to the North of Ratnapura. The road runs through the cheerful Kelani Valley — where hospitable planters abound. The Taldua Club is famous for its Meets — and Drinks. Occasionally the river-god of the Kelani comes up and covers the Club with his waters. Yet the Club emerges — attacked yet intact. Many waters can never quench the Bar.

Here ends our first journey, which can most comfortably be accomplished in two days, and will give a good idea of the many charms of the Southern Province.

Probably you will have taken a great many snapshots on this tour. If so, you can get them speedily and beautifully developed and printed by The Ceylon Arts and Crafts, next to Mackinnon, Mackenzie's, facing the jetty. In photography and cinema-films of Ceylon, you will find this store in the Fort able to satisfy your most urgent demands. On your return home you can show your friends *The Real Ceylon* — in print, and in prints.

The Wild Men of Ceylon

CHAPTER V

This Chapter is mainly concerned with Elephants.

CEYLON without elephants would be like Huntley *minus* Palmer, or a Marshall without his Snelgrove. Veddahs always politely talk of elephants as "They."

This mighty lord of the jungle in India, Burma, and Ceylon is scientifically *Elaphas Indicus;* in Sinhalese, *Allian;* in Tamil, *Yanne.* Indian male elephants usually carry larger tusks than those of Burma and Ceylon. The reason given is that the soil of Ceylon is deficient in lime. The height of an elephant can be easily ascertained, since twice the circumference of the fore-foot, or six times its diameter, gives the height at the shoulder. The biggest elephants in Asia are, males about 9 ft. 10 ins., and females 8 ft. 5 ins. In Ceylon any elephant over 8 ft. 6 ins. is considered a big one. Tuskers are probably only five per cent of the total. Other males have brief apologies for tusks. Once tamed an elephant is a good worker. Recently I saw two elephants pulling out old tea bushes on a steep hillside near Kandapola. Their gift of balance and body-control was amazing. They brought out the bushes, roots and all, with the skill of a dentist!

In Kandyan times the Kings kept specially-trained elephants for the public execution of criminals. The criminal was torn or trampled to death at certain fixed spots at certain times of the year. When the British captured Kandy, the state-execution elephants were turned out into the jungle, as being no longer required: but year after year, they turned up regularly at the fixed times and places, to carry out their duties and be rewarded with a special feed. Eventually, after many disappointments, they disappeared.

The wild herds, as I saw at a Kraal, are invariably led by a female. The tusker "Komban," or the large tuskless "Allian," who rules the herd, travels at the end, or, when resting, in the centre of the herd, for protection, as being the most important member. The sentinels are female elephants, whose duty it is to give the alarm; in which case my lord slips away noiselessly and speedily. There is, by the way, an elephant language, expressed either in shrill trumpeting, deep roaring, or a curious muffled sound made by tapping the ground with the trunk—a signal of great alarm.

Elephants usually feed in the evening and during the night, lying up in dense jungle during the day. They drink only at dawn and sunset, and bathe at night with the regularity of a London clubman! Ceylon elephants are the aristocrats of their kind in Asia. Mrs. Heber records—"The Cingalese affect to say that their superiority is acknowledged by all other elephants, who salaam to them as they pass." Personally, I have not yet observed this pleasing custom in actual practice.

Before you reach Peradeniya Bridge (four miles from Kandy) coming from Colombo, there is a very steep hill to the left,—metalled. I used to wonder how the steam-roller did the job. One day I saw an elephant doing the rolling! Up the hill he laboriously pulled a big stone roller, his trunk round a pole with a cross-piece at the end. At the top, his keeper put a stone under the roller. The elephant then majestically turned round, faced the roller, gripped the cross-piece with his trunk, and, after removal of the stone, cautiously allowed the roller to roll down the hill. Elephants at times become playful. Recently in Negombo an elephant working on the Esplanade suddenly caused a commotion by deserting his mahout and dashing down the crowded main street. The mahout borrowed a bicycle, and caught up the elephant, who went back to work after a lightning strike. This reminds one that at certain seasons elephants "*go must*" and behave riotously. One night a wild elephant did this near a shooting camp. Hurriedly the coolies woke "Master," and begged him to shoot the offender. "Go away," said the sleepy sportsman. "But, Master, elephant *must*" said his boy in great agitation. "Well, tell him he mustn't!" said the weary sportsman, and went to sleep again.

Elephants do varied work. "He will do anything that his keeper bids him, which is possible for a beast not having hands to do." One recently laid the test terminal concrete pole for the Pussellawa automatic telephone system; others shift timber; build stone bridges, take part in *Peraheras*; and possess other diversities of useful gifts. They require about sixty pounds of food a day, consisting of leaves, straw, bamboo shoots and so forth — and gnaw a "bone" at night — a block of fibrous kitul-palm — to keep their teeth in trim. King Raja Singha had specially trained elephants, "appointed all night to stand and watch, lest there should be any tumult; which, if there should, could presently trample down a multitude."

They are very dear creatures, and I am glad to think they are rarely shot nowadays, so long as they are not "proclaimed rogues." On one occasion a wild elephant was rubbing his hind legs against a low forked tree. He got one leg into the fork — where it stuck. He tried for hours to pull his leg out forcibly, but had not the wit to lift his leg and so get clear of the fork. He was shot by villagers.

At night an elephant does not go to bed. He sleeps standing, but never snores; or he may rest his trunk on an ant-hill, so that he is always ready to move off at once, if an alarm is raised, without having to rise up from a recumbent position. As regards age an elephant may live to be 150. One proved example of elephantine longevity can be noted in an elderly elephant who headed the State procession when the Governor, Sir Edward Barnes, after capturing Kandy in 1814, entered the town in procession. In 1890 this historic quadruped was still working on a coconut estate. He was called most appropriately, "Sir Edward Barnes," and was ten feet at the shoulder. Elephants, by the way, hate horses, and dislike small dogs; especially if they sniff at the elephant's hind-legs. So do I. Elephants are rarely bred in captivity, I am told. In Knox's time we read—"Neither will they ever breed tame ones with tame ones; but to ease themselves of the trouble to bring their meat, they will tie their two four-feet together, put them into the woods, where meeting with the wild ones, they conceive and go one year with young."

"Rogue" elephants are mostly solitary males biding their time for mastery over more powerful males actually in possession of a herd of females. The larger a herd, the more powerful the adult male in possession needs to be. If he has tusks, he can hold his position against a much larger male armed only with the abortive tusks, known as "tushes." The natural law of might prevails, and a male, who aspires to dominate a herd, but is unable to do so, is driven out of it, and forced to live a solitary life. This makes him morose in temper, and inclined to find an easy livelihood by depredations on the villagers' rice crops or stacks, from which he is driven off by gunshot wounds by the villagers in their watch-huts in the fields. This in turn makes him vindictive, and apt to maim or kill any villagers who come his way. There are degrees in their mischievousness and danger; but if not destroyed promptly when they evince a determination to injure human beings, they often kill a number of men before they are destroyed themselves. Often an old solitary male is found in company with a younger male. In these cases the younger male acts as sentinel for the old male, and it usually occurs at seasons when the females with young are living apart from the males. When the adult males are living in full association with the herds, the duties of acting as sentinels devolve on the females, whose first duty to the community is the safety of the chief male who, as a rule, is the first to leave the herd on any signal of alarm. It does not sound chivalrous; but it provides for the survival of the member of most importance to the community at the time.

"The people of Ceylon," (writes Haughton) "universally recognize "caste" in elephants; projecting their own ingrained ideas into other animals, especially the lordly elephant. The highest caste elephants are what are called "white" elephants; they are covered with large irregular pinkish-white blotches on the head, ears, and trunk, and are greatly prized by the people. A good caste elephant is of well-shaped head, strong compact body, with stout legs and feet; latter of good diameter. The circular fore-feet should contain five good-sized handsome nails, all resting on the ground, and the oval hind-feet four nails. His eyes should be the colour of honey. Low-caste elephants are lanky, long-legged animals, with small feet and black skin." King Raja Singha had a much-prized "*Elephant* spotted or speckled all the body over, which was lately caught; and tho' he hath many and very stately *Elephants*, and may have as many more as he pleases, yet he prefers this before them all."

Except in the case of "rogue" elephants and herd elephants trespassing on cultivated lands, wild elephants are not otherwise mischievous, though from curiosity and lightness of heart they at times exhibit a certain liveliness by pulling up milestones or tilting their foreheads against newly made earth-work on village tanks or public works, apparently to see how far they can drive their heads into the clay. A small herd once found a canoe full of baggage in a river mouth and shoved it a long way on the muddy bank of the river. I should imagine elephants enjoy April the first with rural pranks.

As regards elephant shooting, in olden days this was freely indulged in, largely to protect the crops of villagers. Now, a costly licence must, very properly, be obtained; and only an occasional foreigner shoots an elephant as part of his grand tour. I may perhaps quote, as an example, Haughton's adventure in an encounter with a fighting female.

"The jungle was, if possible, getting worse, and when heading cautiously in the direction of the "rogue" we were unexpectedly charged in the flank by an enormous infuriated female elephant about eight feet high. (Such females are extremely dangerous, and even the most courageous and skilful trappers give them a wide berth). She did not see us at first (I had a green suit on, the same colour as the jungle), and charged madly round us, only smelling us. My first shot in the temple wheeled her round, and she charged again close to us from another direction. I then hit her with a second shot from the heavy rifle, again in the head; but this time the heavy jungle branches deflected the bullet, which only hit her in the lower jaw. This stopped her, and I threw down my rifle and snatched the second gun (a heavy No. 12 smooth-bore) from my man, but seeing that the elephant was stunned and that she did not yet see us, I stooped down and snatched up the heavy rifle and reloaded it, and as I closed the breech hurriedly, the noise was heard by her, and she then knew our exact position. Dripping with blood and more infuriated than ever, with raised head and curled-up trunk, she came right down on top of us. It was an anxious moment, and if I failed to stop her, death for one or both of us seemed certain, as she had seen us and was raging. Just as she commenced her charge, I bettered my position by a step to one side, and took a glance at my black companion. He was cool and true at my left hand, though green with fright, and the blood jumped through his neck as if it would split his skin. As she crashed down on us within ten yards I fired my next shot in the right temple, and it was with intense relief I saw her fall forward within a few feet of the end of my rifle on her knees and forehead. Hurrying to her side, I fired another through the head as she was struggling to regain her feet, and a final shot from the smoothbore in her ear ended the encounter. I never in all my life went through a livelier time, and I don't want to encounter such another furious brute again in a hurry. After I was all over, I felt sick and faint for a while, though I was cool and steady while it lasted."

The Veddahs usually talk of elephants as "They." They make good mothers. Knox, says "The Chingulayes report, they bear the greatest love to their young of all irrational creatures; for the shees are alike tender of any one's young ones as of their own: when there are many she-elephants together, the young ones go and suck of any, as well of their mothers; and if a young one be in distress and should cry out, they will all in general run to the help and aid thereof; and if they be going over a river, as here be some somewhat broad, and the streams run very swift, they will with all their trunks assist and help to carry the young ones over."

At a Kraal I saw a sad sight. A baby-elephant, born during the drive-in, was crushed to death in a pool. The mother went away in a rush, and came back to find her baby dead. When she realised the truth, her grief was terrible to behold.

There is a lovely valley with a trout-stream at Ambawela, the next station to Nanu-Oya. In the jungle above this stream live a herd of elephants, about 36 in all. They intensely dislike intrusion. Once the Ceylon Fishing Club imported at great expense from home a number of freshwater crabs to improve the food supply in the stream. The crabs, for protection, were enclosed in wire-covered cages, so that they might breed and multiply. The cages were secured in the middle of the stream. The next night the elephants came down and smashed the cages to bits. They would not tolerate interference in their waters like this. On another occasion, during the breeding-season, two fishermen, Hill and Shelley by name, went rather near the ladies. An old elephant gave chase. Hill dashed into the river and watched Shelley, a notable sprinter, being chased. Luckily, the elephant had only one eye. Suddenly Hill saw the elephant turn a double somersault, not having seen an ant-hill in his way. So Shelley escaped. Hill used to say he never saw an animal look more surprised than that elephant did after taking such an almighty toss.

The Fishing Club has built a hut near the stream in memory of that great sportsman, Wallis-Wilson. Round the hut is a deep ditch. Access is afforded by a light bridge that no elephant would cross. Otherwise that hut would soon be destroyed. "They" hate trespassers.

Every school-boy ought (if he knows Sanskrit) to read a work by Nilakantha in 263 stanzas dealing with Elephants, their ways and works. An English translation has been published under the title, "The Elephant-lore of the Hindus." In South India you can purchase little red seeds with white lids inserted. If you peep inside, you may find from one up to fifty tiny white ivory elephants hiding inside. Peter Stagg (aged six) and I once asked them how they got there.

We do it thus, they all explained, when elephants must die.
They go and find a Bury-Tree, and under it they lie;
And lying very, very, still, they neither eat nor drink,
But die in peace and start to shrink,
and shrink,
and shrink,
and shrink.

So that is why no one ever sees a dead elephant in the jungle. At least, that is what Peter says.

I will end by quoting a pithy Sinhalese proverb:

Before catching elephants, plan not the work to be done by them.

I have no space to write much about all the other beasts, gentle or ferocious, of the jungle, whose law is "*Eat, or be eaten.*" Leopards abound. Rarely one becomes, like the famous Leopard of Punani, a man-killer. This beast disposed of at least fifteen people before a planter slew him. He specially enjoyed killing postmen. I wish I had space to tell the manner of his being killed at last. Panthers are not so common, and are rarely seen. I have been at night near Habarane within forty feet of a leopard on the road, and had to blow my horn twice to dislodge him. The Ceylon bear (*Ursus labiatus*) is a foul animal, not averse to carrion. His coat is coarse, thin, and mangy. His claws are long and deadly, but useful for digging. His lips are large and help him to extract honey from rocks and hollows. The Ceylon bear — especially if a female with young — is ferocious and attacks without provocation. I once saw a villager with half his face clawed off: yet he recovered. A high Ceylon official was once severely injured out on circuit. In jungle surgery such a wound is stitched up with sharp thorns, where no medical skill is available: and people recover! Most accidents (happily they are not common) occur when villagers are hunting for honey in the jungle, and happen to meet a bear suddenly in a narrow path. At night if you motor slowly along a jungle road you may see one ambling along. Anything in fur in the tropics looks out of place.

As regards deer — which are quite often seen from cars in jungle parts — the Sambur (often in Ceylon called the Elk) is the largest, reaching thirty stones in weight. They are hunted in the hills by mixed packs, and usually knifed when brought to a standstill by the "seizers" — big hounds trained for this dangerous task.

The wild boar is common, and does much damage to the villager's crops. Crocodiles abound in many parts: at Puttalam they are harmless, and you can see crowds bathing close to a number of crocks. Crocodiles never go to a dentist. They have an endless succession of new teeth, unlike human old crocks. They lay eggs, which are hatched out on land and little crocs emerge 9 inches long. They have the full number of teeth on emerging from the egg, yet gentle little birds hop about in their mouths picking bits of meat from beneath the teeth. No wonder a bird needs 95% of courage in its make-up, and only 5% of matter.

Smaller animals sometimes seen are Leopard-cats, Jungle-cats, Civet-cats, Jackals, tiny Mouse Deer, and Hares — some times black-necked. There are no wild rabbits in Ceylon, happily. The chief game-birds are Pea-fowl, Jungle-fowl, Partridge, Quail. The Jungle-fowl are lovely birds, and excellent to eat, if not too old. So are Pea-fowl. The game-birds on tanks and in marshes are Duck (of many kinds) Teal, Mallard, and Snipe (from September to May). You will often see a mongoose cross the road, eternally hunting. He is the sworn foe of the deadly snakes — Cobras and Tic Polongas. One rarely sees these snakes, as a matter of fact.

As regards birds, their name is legion. I will only name a few:—

Pelican, Flamingo, Water-Pheasant, Hornbill, Oriole, Paradise-Flycatcher, Cuckoo, Myna, Weaver-Bird, Hoopoo, Devil-Bird, Woodpecker, Kingfisher, Magpie-Robin, and King Crow.

To see a Flamingo family in flight at sunrise or sunset is to see a miracle of winged beauty—their pink and white plumage alternately changing—a very lovely sight.

The golden roads to Trincomalee and Batticaloa provide these wonders of nature in profusion. Personally, I never tire

Old Palace, Kandy.

Fishing—Nuwara Eliya.

of watching them at work, at love, or at play. Of the King-Crow, this jungle-myth is worth quoting:

Would you like to find The Philosopher's Stone in Lanka? If so, find a place in the jungle where three streams meet. Two streams will be found flowing down-hill, and one up-hill. Follow the stream flowing up-hill till you meet a very thorny bush. Thrust your hand into this bush, and try to find a King-Crow's nest in the centre.

Then — the Philosopher's stone will, infallibly, be found in the nest.

In conclusion, remember one thing. You may not actually with your eyes see many wild creatures in the jungle; but millions of eyes are watching you all the time. Every action of man is closely scrutinised by a great cloud of invisible wild witnesses—especially monkeys.

In the new Colombo Zoological Gardens you may see in captivity many of the animals I have mentioned. But, to my mind, one wild animal seen at liberty in the jungle is worth a whole collection in cages, however excellent.

You will probably take home an Elephant — in ebony. It is a pity that the anatomy of these charming souvenirs is so defective as regards their hind-legs and toe-nails.

CHAPTER VI

THE KINGDOM OF KANDY

IN the year 1660 a shipman, named Captain Robert Knox, was wrecked on the East coast of Ceylon and, after capture, taken to Kandy as a prisoner. He finally escaped after exciting adventures to the West coast in the year 1680 and reached England. He was a man gifted with keen powers of observation, and master of a sound style in English. He published in 1681 his famous book entitled :—

AN
HISTORICAL RELATION
OF THE ISLAND,
CEYLON,
1681.

So we are fortunate in having an intimate picture of Kandy as seen from the inside in the seventeenth century. A cheap edition of the book has lately been published, and is most excellent reading. I have borrowed freely, like every other writer on Ceylon, from Knox's famous volume.

Kandy is 72 miles by road from Colombo, and is about 1,500 feet above sea-level. The road from Colombo to Kandy is full of historical interest. It was opened in 1822, and in 1832 a mail coach started running, *"the first mail coach in Asia."*

Along this road British troops in scarlet with stiff stocks and high gaiters and huge shakos tramped stolidly — the P.B.I. of their age. The big Rest-houses at Mahara and Ambepusse no doubt provided quarters *en route*. It is interesting about the 17th mile post to examine a stone of warning marked "DEEP WATER." The exhausted private jumped in, apparently, for a swim and met his death. For in the old Ceylon papers I have found records of soldiers drowned near the Kandy road.

One thinks with admiration of the curricles, bandies, and palanquins that so long dotted its dusty surface. A palanquin, in those days, required 13 servants. *"Only four,"* we read, *"carry at a time: but they are relieved every quarter-of-an-hour, and shift the pole from the shoulder of one to the shoulder of another without stopping. The 13th man acts as a cook to the set and carries all the culinary apparatus."*

The first Cook's tour!

Kegalle has the remains of an old Fort defended by a solitary surviving cannon. Further on to the left is the famous Sardiel's Rock. Sardiel was the Robin Hood of the 'fifties — or, less picturesquely, the last of the brigands. He was finally captured on his rock at night by a young Civil Servant (better known afterwards as Sir Frederick Saunders). Found guilty of murder he was hanged in Kandy gaol. The Rev. F. D. Waldock once told me about the brigand's closing days in prison. He said Sardiel listened courteously to him when expounding the tenets of Christianity, but stoutly refused to change his faith. He was a Buddhist, like most Kandyans.

Further on to the right, one sees the Bible Rock — a square booky-looking mass. Then high up to the left is the granite mass of Allagalle, from the summit of which in the old days criminals were hurled to their doom. On the Kadugannawa Pass is the ancient rock, pierced by the road-making British, thus fulfilling the ancient prophecy that when that rock was vanquished Kandyan domination would cease. At the top is the Dawson Monument, commemorating the opening of the road.

I do not propose to tell of the many bitter and bloody wars fought by the Kandyans against Portuguese, Dutch, and British forces in turn, with varying success along this road, and elsewhere. Suffice it to say that the conquest of the Kingdom of Kandy was finally effected by General Brownrigg on February 19th, 1815. Kandy in the end fell from within.

"From this day," wrote Knighton, *"we may date the extinction of Ceylonese independence: an independence which had continued without any material interruption for 2357 years."* On March 6th after surrender, the King of Kandy and his family arrived in Colombo as State prisoners. The prison house, already referred to, was *"spacious and handsomely fitted up."* On entering the King observed, "As I am no longer permitted to be a King, I am thankful for the kindness and attention which have been shown to me." He was the last of a line of 165 Kings.

A solemn convention was held in the Audience-Hall of the Palace on March 2nd, 1815, between the Governor of Ceylon and the Adikars, Dissaves, and other principal Kandyan Chiefs.

The Treaty confirming the annexation was read by Mr. Sutherland, Deputy-Secretary to Government in English and then in Sinhalese, and King George III thus became Sovereign of the whole Island of Ceylon. The Treaty expressly stated that:—

"The religion of Boodhoo, professed by the Chiefs and inhabitants of the Kandyan provinces, is declared inviolable, and its rites, ministers, and places of worship, are to be maintained and protected."

I quote a passage from Marshall:—

"By this memorable proclamation or convention, it appears that the English Government recognises and adopts the principle of making sovereigns accountable for their abuse of the power entrusted to them, the King of Kandy being dethroned for misgovernment, cashiered for offences committed against his subjects, called to account for his actions, and punished for abuse of power."

Marshall met the deposed King, and describes him as "about five feet nine or ten inches in height, slightly corpulent, stoutly made, and muscular. He had a pleasant expression of countenance, a handsome beard, broad shoulders, and a full chest. His figure was manly, and his general appearance dignified. He did not appear to the writer to be deficient in intellect, and was generally much more affable and good-humoured than could be expected of a deposed king in a state of confinement."

Cordiner describes the King as "a young Malabar of inferior extraction and no talents." But in fact the King was a cadet of the Royal House of Madura in South India, and, after being elevated to the throne by his ministers, displayed considerable gifts. Like many other Oriental Kings he was "a despot by condition and necessity," and ruled according to his lights. In Knox's Ceylon you will read enough to show what those lights were.

After crossing the Mahaweli Ganga — Ceylon's greatest river, that runs into the sea near Trincomalee — we pass the famous Peradeniya Botanical Gardens on our left, with the comfortable, well-run Rest-house opposite, where the Butler provides savoury curry and rice, (if you ask for it), as weli as tasty, well-cooked English dishes. Curry, by the way, is the Portuguese word *Carree,* meaning relish. Rice, of course, is rice. Ask always, by the way, for "Country Rice."

Three miles further on we enter Kandy. I once defined this famous little Township as "a spiritual expression in a physical depression." The Temple of the Sacred Tooth (Dalade Maligawa) is the central feature, though in my humble opinion the huge new erection at the back, however necessary for practical purposes, has rather spoiled the Temple from the aesthetic point of view. I will now (thanks to the courtesy of the Government Agent, Mr. Dyson and Mrs. Dyson) take you to the Old Palace, the official residence of the Head of the Central Province. The existing buildings formed part of the ancient Royal Palace, housing the royal ladies. They were not kept in *purdah,* and a series of small square windows set in line enabled them to see the ceremonies in the Temple close by. The interior of the old Palace has a very lovely room, as the pictures show, with a big entrance door in the graceful Kandyan style: and the long verandah is a noble feature. The walls inside are decorated with Kandyan figures and heraldic beasts in relief, giving a delightfully archaic effect. Some day, probably, the old Palace will be turned into a Kandyan Museum, and might then house the throne and Regalia. Mrs. Heber in her Journal wrote a description of the Palace worth quoting :—

"We dined in the King's Palace with Mr. and Mrs. Downing. This is a very long low building, at the extremity of the town, painted white with stone gateways; its front extending nearly two hundred yards; a hexagonal building of two stories terminates it at one end, in which we were received; the rooms we saw are small and low, with curious grotesque figures carved on the walls. Here the Monarch used to show himself in State to his people, with a wife on either hand; for, though the Kandyan females of rank have seldom been seen by Europeans, they were not before the conquest kept in seclusion."

Mrs. Heber then describes the Temple and other features of Kandy graphically. She wields a lively pen and her whole Journal is definitely feminine but interesting.

The Audience-Hall, notable for the skilful carving of the pillars, and typical steeply pitched roof, remains: and is used by the Supreme Court on circuit for criminal trials. The King's Palace (of which it formed part) is no longer in existence. In this Hall the Kandy Convention was published. Here I saw his late Majesty King Edward VII, when Prince of Wales, hold a great Durbar, which was attended by the Kandyan Chiefs in all their glory — a very beautiful and historic sight. In front of the Audience-Hall of those days was a great square, which is now much curtailed. The King of Kandy rarely used the great Audience-Hall, as he usually preferred to sit cross-legged on an elevated throne on occasions of ceremony in a room adjoining. That room no longer exists. I might mention that by ancient custom Kandyan courtiers from time immemorial withdrew from the Presence on all-fours. Ambassadors greeted him on their knees.

Mrs. Heber describes how on Sunday, September 18th, 1825, Bishop Heber held a confirmation-service in the Audience-Hall and preached a long sermon. Here the good lady indulges in some moral reflections of a most elevating type: but, for the wife of a Bishop, she on the whole is a most sensible woman.

Visitors who see the Governor's stately residence, the Pavilion, in Kandy, will read with interest that in 1825 it consisted of "a small cluster of bungalows dignified by the name of The Pavilion."

From the point of view of personal comfort, the traveller will find in Kandy a most delightful Hotel called The Suisse. It is charmingly situated on an eminence overlooking the lake. I can suggest no more pleasant experience than a week-end spent here in Kandy — "the little town in a big green saucer" as one might define it. All round are glorious walks and drives, and the cool atmosphere is a welcome relief to residents after the higher temperatures of the Low-country. Kandy is the recognised centre of the planters — a very fine body of hard-working men, who have contributed, and still contribute, so much to the stability and prosperity of the Island. Their hospitality is prodigious: they foster every kind of sport: and, for remuneration that is often inadequate, they render great service in every field — social, sporting, agricultural, and, now, political. They have fine headquarters and an excellent Club in the heart of the town.

Now we come to the Temple of the Sacred Tooth. Here I wish to express my indebtedness to the present Kachcheri Mudaliyar at Kandy, Mr. K. B. Wijekoon, who has given me valuable help and information, as follows :—

The famous little Temple, called Dalada (Tooth) Maligawa (Temple) stands on the North side of the Lake. Its history is interesting.

King Wimala Dharma Suriya II (A.D. 1687-1707) built a temple of three storeys, and, when it was decayed, his son King Narendra Sinha (A.D. 1707-1739) rebuilt it with the two storeys which exist to-day. It is in this building that the left eye-tooth of Gautama Buddha is enshrined.

Ecclesiastically, this Temple is in charge of the Siamese Sect of the Buddhist priests. There are two monasteries belonging to this sect known as Malwatta and Asgiriya, situated some distance from the Temple. The priests of this sect are men of good families, for they do not admit any one below the *goigama* caste into their priesthood. Each community has a Maha Nayaka (Chief High-Priest) and each community in turn is in charge of the temple. The two Maha Nayakas alternately appoint three priests for the performance of the rites (*Thevava*) for the year. They change at the full moon day of the month of Esala (June-July). Two of these priests are for the up-stair sanctuary, and the other for the lower-floor shrine. The .priest in the lower-floor has no authority to officiate in the upper floor; but the priests in the upper-floor can officiate in the lower-floor in the absence of the officiating priest. During their term of office, the priests live in the Pansala (dwelling-quarter) in the South side of the Temple.

The Temple is controlled by a layman, bearing the title of Diyawadana Nilame. In ancient days the King always appointed him; but now he is elected by the two Maha Nayakas of Malwatta and Asgiriya, Adigars, Dissawas, (those holding honorary Kandyan rank), Ratemahatmayas, (Chief Headmen), Basnayake Nilames (Temple Chiefs), and trustees of temples having an annual income of Rs. 1,000 in the Kandyan Provinces. The Diyawadana

Nilame administers the revenue of the temple, appoints the minor officials, and carries out the festivities connected with the Temple. He is usually called "The Diya Nilame." The present occupant, recently elected, is a member of the Ratwatte family.

When a new Diyawadana Nilame is appointed, an auspicious day and hour are chosen for the Tooth Relic to be handed over ceremoniously into his custody. This is done in the Shrine Room by the Maha Nayakas of Asgiriya and Malwatte. Rosewater is sprinkled by the two High Priests on the palms of the new Diya Nilame, and then the sacred Relic placed on a silken handkerchief is handed over. The Diya Nilame receives the relic and elevates it to his head as an act of worship. Outside in the courtyard below special religious dances are performed by Kandyan dancers to the sound of the tom-tom. Later the Temple treasures are checked and handed over to the new Diya Nilame, and his installation is complete.

The Temple officials are called Atul Kattale Rajakariya karana aya (*The Performers of service of the inner shrine*). The chief of the minor officials is known as Karia Korala. He supervises all the services of the Temple, and notifies all the tenants of the various festivals, so that they may perform their share of the service. All these officials and the tenants hold land for their services according to Kandyan Law.

The Tooth Relic is in the joint custody of the two Maha Nayakas and the Diyawadana Nilame. The room up-stairs, in which the Tooth Relic is kept, is known as Vedasitina Maligawa (*the Shrine of Abode*). In this room the Tooth is kept, enclosed by gilt iron bars fixed into the back wall. There is only one key for this iron cage, and it is held by the Diyawadana Nilame. The Tooth Relic is enclosed in seven caskets, one inside the other; there are three sets of keys for these caskets — one with the Diyawadana Nilame, and one with each of the Maha Nayakas. The seven caskets can only be opened when all three high officials are present.

The treasures of the Temple are many and beautiful. I shall never forget the occasion when I was privileged to be present and to examine them quietly. The picture of the Sacred Tooth gives the exact size. Of the treasures, I liked best the crystal image of Buddha; but all the other treasures are worthy of most prolonged examination. The official list is as follows :—

1. The casket in which the Tooth Relic is taken in Perahera. It is of gold and covered with cat's-eyes and other gems.
2. One casket presented by the Government of India along with the relics found in the Dharmarajika stupa in Taxila.
3. Seven caskets in which the Tooth Relic is deposited.
4. Crystal image of Buddha.
5. A fan of solid gold set with jewels.
6. A solid gold betel stand (Dalumura tattuwa) covered with jewels. This was presented by the mother of King Kirthi Sri Raja Sinha, and it bears an inscription to the effect that it was used by her and presented to the temple.
7. One small flower tray made of gold given by King Kirthi Sri.
8. One large flower-tray made of gold and silver. It was presented by Sir Edward Barnes, (Governor of Ceylon from 1824-1831) to a Kandyan Chief, who presented it to the Temple.
9. A silver spittoon.
10. Two golden Kendiyas (vessels to hold water).
11. One kuda dharsana, long chain with pendants attached, presented by King Kirthi Sri.
12. One maha dharsana, long chain with pendants attached, presented by King Kirthi Sri.
13. Several golden bowls (*patras*).
14. Various items of jewelry.
15. Several caskets and images of Buddha.
16. Other valuable offerings made by the Buddhists of Burma.

In 1898 I happened to be in Kandy when the great gift from Burma arrived, valued at £60,000. Customs duty on this gift was a large amount, which was paid by an eminent Buddhist, the late Mr. Mututantrige Simon Fernando Sri Chandrasekera

Mudaliyar, of Horekele, near Panadure. I knew him well, and always found him a most satisfactory client! A local Sinhalese poet has described the occasion lyrically :—

Behold!

A costly shrine from Burma was landed in Lanka.

Unhappily the Customs duty to be paid was immense. Wonderful to relate, the Deity that protects the Buddhist religion brought this great Personage hither, and the money was duly paid.

The act of this Mudaliyar in handing over the shrine to contain the Tooth Relic is like a flag to the Peoples of Lanka.

Seed sown in a fertile field yields good crops. Meritorial acts, done with pious zeal, grow daily, and bestow rewards on children and grand-children.

Learn the way to do acts of merit from this book-like Personage.

In the Temple Library, the delightful octagonal room overlooking the green, you will find many very old manuscripts inscribed on *olas* (palm leaves) in Pali and Sanskrit. This quiet retreat is perhaps seen to perfection at dusk, when the tom-toms of the Temple sound the call to evening prayer.

As an instrument of music the tom-tom is universally popular in Ceylon — and rightly so. It plays a great part in religion, medicine, drama, sport, and music. Heard at a distance from cooly-lines on a tea-estate it blends naturally with the atmosphere, and has real charm. At close range, however, it might become monotonous. Lest you should think that tom-tom playing is simple let an expert instruct us :—

"Playing the tom-tom is a serious art. The players approach it with reverence. Once you learn to perform on it you will find in it as good rhythm and harmony as in any other musical instrument.

It is not mere hammering away on a skin-covered wooden tube. You start your lessons (which are many and more varied than with the piano) with *"denktu denkutu kendata polkudu"* and gradually finish up with *"thana tha than thanta thana na na."*

Cast not away the remnants of a national heritage for the sake of protecting uneducated eardrums."

If you watch the chief musician of the troupe of Kandyan dancers organised by Mr. Ellawalla, you will see this art demonstrated to perfection by a great master of tintinnabulation, and an actor of long experience.

To the west of the Dalada Maligawa is the Natha Devala. It stands on a raised enclosure. Besides the shrine of the Bodhisattva, the terrace contains a small *stupa,* in which, by tradition, is deposited the bowl-relic (*patra dhatu*) of the Buddha. The shrine is the only building in Kandy made entirely of stone. The date of this building is unknown. It is well worth a visit. It is probably the earliest historical building extant in Kandy. In the Perahera the second place of honour is given to the image of Natha. At this shrine the King of Kandy chose his propitious official name, and was girded with the regal sword, by a member of the Pilimi Talauva family. Here also at the New Year did the royal physicians prepare 1,000 pots of medicinal ointments made of wild herbs, which were supplied for the use of the Royal Family and High Priests of various temples.

Of the great Perahera held in August each year, I could write much, did space permit. It is a fine sight to see the specially chosen elephant enter the Temple Gate, and majestically ascend the steps to receive upon his gaily-caparisoned back the Sacred Shrine, which is taken in procession through the streets of Kandy, with a great multitude of worshippers adoring. Kandyan dancers, torch-bearers, musicians, and flag-bearers, and perhaps a hundred elephants make up a stirring processional picture never to be forgotten. The festival lasts for days. With Wesak in May (the birthday of Buddha), Poson in June (the advent of Buddhism to Ceylon), and the August Perahera, the three great festivals are celebrated by Buddhists. But at every season of the year Kandy, and its leafy environs, offers great attractions to travellers.

"See Naples and die!" said an enthusiast long ago.

"See Kandy and dream!" is my motto.

For Kandy fills the soul with the waters of peace and reflection. I often wish I could have visited it with Fa-Hien. When he reached the Hall on Mount Gridhrakuta in India, where Buddha preached his law, Fa-Hien fell sad, but restrained his tears and said :—

"Here Buddha delivered his doctrine. I, Fa-Hien, was born when I could not meet Buddha, and now I only see the footprints that he left and the place where he lived, and nothing more."

Kandy makes one feel like that at times. Buddha, (whose family name was Gautama) means "*The Enlightened One.*" What the world wants to-day is More Light.

Since funeral rites were always regarded by Kandyans as a solemn duty, I might mention the *Adhahara-Maluwa* (*the Place of Burning*) where only the highest of the Royal Dead, the King, his mother, and his elder sister left their ashes. The spot is at the foot of the hill leading up to the Asgiri Vihare, near the road to Peradeniya. On the death of a King, a Herald entered a funeral-house erected outside the Audience Hall, and gave a public signal to the Court by beating upon the mourning tom-tom; commanded all Chiefs to be clad in black garments; and solemnly proclaimed the King's successor. The funeral rites thereafter were celebrated with great dignity, and for 11 days the funeral pyre was kept burning. Finally the ashes were cast into the Mahaweli Ganga near Katugastotte. Court mourning lasted for one month; but till his ceremonial coronation the King wore a black handkerchief round his head To-day nothing remains of the royal burying ground, save a round stone that was part of the top of the Dagaba over the grave of Kirthi Sri, and a few steps.

There sle the Kings of Kandy, and will sleep, until :—

The dead shall live; the dead bodies shall arise.
Awake and sing, ye that dwell in the dust; for thy dew
is as the dew of herps. and the Earth shall give up her dead.

CHAPTER VII

ON TANKS AND DAGABAS

JOHN STILL in *The Jungle Tide* has pointed out that Ceylon has two distinct climatic zones — one wet and the other dry. The dividing line, drawn by the Creator, depicts on a map exactly where the difference lies. The seasonal rains, called Monsoons, supply the water from the South-West and North-East in turn, starting usually in June and October.

In China the sign of an upright cross (or *plus* sign in arithmetic) is the chief part of the character for rice; which *"is the immortal nourishing Child of Heaven and thus meaneth life."* Accordingly in the dry zone of Lanka (mainly in the Northern, North-Central and Eastern Provinces) where the bulk of the population lived in ancient days, Kings thought and took counsel with their officers of State largely in terms of food. Hence came the wonderful ancient system of "tanks" — great reservoirs in which the water was stored up, and then distributed by channels to the thirsting sun-baked rice-fields. For rice was life: without rice, famine — death One must bear this in mind when visiting the above-mentioned Provinces, the home formerly of myriads — now sparsely inhabited, and to-day famous chiefly for the so-called Buried Cities of Ceylon. But, remember, the lost cities were many — such as Tambaponni and Wijita. The Buried Cities of to-day by no means exhaust the list. Tambaponni, for example, was the Capital of Vijaya — *"the first city of the excellent Island of Lanka."* To-day not one stone remains of a great city.

Population in ancient Lanka followed water; and so a study of the earliest irrigation works of ancient Ceylon is a most absorbing one. Mr. Parker, who was for years in the Irrigation Department of Ceylon, deals fully with this fascinating subject in his *Ancient Ceylon*. The Giant's Tank (literally *Giant-built Embankment*) is one of the best known, and very ancient. In and around Anuradhapura are many fine tanks such as Tissa Wæwa, and Nuwara Wæwa. The river Kadamba (now called the Malwatta-oya,) runs through the city, and was an important feature of the system of irrigation. Many inscriptions record how kings restored tanks: *The Mahavansa* (the great Sinhalese chronicle) describes, for example, the re-construction of "The great Uruwela tank" by Parakrama Bahu I. Usually the benefactor left a record of his work carved upon a stone pillar, giving the date and details.

As regards construction of buildings, usually the first storey was of brick or stone, the upper storeys being of wood. It is curious that the histories compiled in early times by monks contain few references to the building of tanks — policies of life-insurance in a literal sense. The first notice of a tank in Ceylon is found in *The Mahavansa,* where it is recorded that Prince Anuradha built a tank on the southern side of the capital some 400 years B.C. Presumably tanks were so well-known and so common that the monks deemed it unnecessary to write much about them.

On examining maps of Ceylon it will be seen that the ancient cities usually lay in shallow valleys down which flowed seasonal streams of moderate size, and so enjoyed a heavy rainfall for a short period. To hold up and conserve the water, the Sinhalese masons skilfully raised huge earthen embankments, often miles in length, intercepting the flow of streams and thus storing up in tanks immense sheets of water for the irrigation of lower-lying tracts of rice-fields. After the introduction of Buddhism, irrigated lands were often donated for the maintenance of the Priesthood, and thus it was a pious act to construct such public works. In time, little communal tanks were constructed at every town or village in the drier districts. One sees remains of them everywhere — some in a sad state of disrepair. This idea of the conservation of water probably originated in the Euphrates Valley; was copied in South India; and thence transmitted to Ceylon. Visitors will specially enjoy the view from the "bund" of Kanthalai tank, along which runs the road to Trincomalee. On these tanks bird-life is gloriously profuse and beautiful. Many are covered with water-lilies of various kinds and colours.

II

Most countries have peculiar forms of construction for places of burial. Egypt has the four-sided pyramid. In Ceylon the lovely form is called the Dagaba. The word Dagaba is akin to

Pagoda, signifying Relic-Shrine. Tradition tells us that the earliest Dagaba built in Ceylon was at Mahiyangana in Eastern Ceylon during the lifetime of Buddha, in order to enshrine a handful of his sacred hair. But, historically, the erection of the first Dagaba took place in the reign of Devanampiya Tissa (B.C. 245). This is the famous Thuparama Dagaba at Anuradhapura, which was founded to enshrine two relics of Buddha — his right collar-bone, and the plate off which he ate his rice. On top of the dome was a flat square of masonry, with a cylinder, from which rose the graceful spire. Around the base was a circular-paved court-yard (164½ feet in diameter, raised 11½ feet above the adjoining ground), to which two sets of graceful steps gave access. The small chamber in which the relics of Buddha were placed was in the upper part of the dome. Later Kings further embellished this Dagaba. A golden pinnacle was affixed to the spire by one king about A.D. 380, but removed by another king about A.D. 650. A sub-king called Karsapa once stole from this Dagaba the sacred relics and gems placed in it, but the Dagaba was restored later. When Karsapa ascended the throne, he placated the Priesthood by adding a pinnacle studded with gems. I can only mention one other famous Dagaba, the Ruwanwaeli Dagaba at Anuradhapura, partially built by King Duttha-Gemini (161-137 B.C.) and completed by his successor. Hundreds of other Dagabas, great and small, were built by pious Kings, more or less upon the lines already mentioned. Many of them, which had fallen into decay, have been restored recently by pious Buddhists. A notable example is the recent restoration of the massive Ruwanwaeli Dagaba.

As for these stately edifices, are not their glories written in the Sinhalese Chronicles with such a wealth of detail that I need not dwell further upon them here? The Abhayagiri Dagaba, built in B.C. 137, is the largest of all. I might mention that the shape of the Ruwanwaeli Dagaba is picturesquely explained in *The Mahavansa.* The King enquired of the builder in what form he would construct it.

"The bricklayer, filling a golden dish with water, and taking some water in the palm of his hand, dashed it against the water in the dish, so that a great globule like a ball of crystal rose to the surface. 'In this form,' said the bricklayer, 'will I construct it.' The King, being delighted, bestowed on this bricklayer a valuable garment, a pair of slippers and 12,000 kahapanas."

It was indeed a bubble-reputation! Parker's dry comment is — "At the present day, even the slippers are not given to successful architects in Ceylon."

The unsuccessful ones, of course, get the boot.

Anciently there were recognised canons of art in design and construction practised by builders of Dagabas. A manuscript has been found in which the received ideas were collected about the 5th Century A.D. Here the various proportions and units are meticulously laid down, and all Dagabas were classified by reference to the shape of the dome, which might be :—

1. Bell. 2. Chatty (pot). 3. Bubble. 4. Heap-of-Paddy 5. Lotus. 6. Nelli (fruit).

The wanderer in Ceylon may find pleasure in classifying the Dagabas seen, according to this canon. Modern designs still conform to ancient observances as regards shapes, and heights of dome and *Chatta*.

The relic-rooms, containing valuable gifts, were often rifled by impious treasure-seekers, who cut their way through the upper part of the dome. In the Dhatuvansa is an interesting account of how a King and Queen enriched the Seruvila Dagaba, built to enshrine the forehead-relic and the hair-relic of Buddha. The King carried the forehead-relic ceremoniously on his head, and the Queen next deposited the hair-relic in the chamber. Afterwards all nobles and other persons presented as pious offerings the jewellery and ornaments that they were wearing. Finally the chamber was tightly closed by being covered by a great stone slab. Often you will see a seven-headed cobra carved on a pillar to serve as a guard to the whole structure and the relics it contained. Sometimes rows of elephants' heads were carved in stone, projecting from the plain course above the lowest cornice of the Wahalkada. These dignified objects were put there for protective purposes, as being auspicious, and therefore to be avoided by evil spirits. Rectangular stone flower-altars were set up at the four cardinal points, as floral offerings formed an important part of Temple ritual, and still do to-day. Every Dagaba had its special flower garden, carefully tended, producing roses, jasmines, and other scented blossoms in profusion.

By courtesy *The Ceylon Tea Propaganda Board.*

Elephant Bathing.

By courtesy *The Ceylon Tea Propaganda Board.*

Sigiriya Rock.

For myself, I never weary of gazing quietly at these great monuments of piety, which are the most notable of Ceylon's architectural splendours. When you come on a huge Dagaba suddenly — partly ruined, in the jungle — you are reminded of Ruskin's emotions on first seeing St. Mark's Cathedral at Venice. These Dagabas so stately, so immense, so beautifully proportioned, in a setting of green jungle, give one a sense of spiritual satisfaction. I like Parker's thoughts on such a building: "The appearance of the great white dome covered with plaster and of this high spire towering aloft in the blue sky, with its gilded upper chattas reflecting the bright rays of the tropical sun, must have been extremely effective and picturesque. It was a striking memorial of its great rounder, and of the artistic genius of the Sinhalese race."

Very literally are Dagabas sermons in brick and stone.

Lately I have made several trips to our 'Unburied Cities' (as I prefer to call them) after a period of several years. The improvement is great, thanks to the cultural labours of Mr. Longhurst, Director of Archæology, and his gifted staff. Unshapely mounds of old are now wisely restored to something like what they were long ago. For example, at Polonnaruwa to-day the Queen's Bath has been turned from a pit of desolation to its former glory. Roads such as were laid out by former Kings have been re-opened, and one sees the great city of Polonnaruwa in all her glory of grey stone and green verdure once more. To me, these Memorials of long Ago, are now more beautiful than ever. In Anuradhapura the problem is harder; for Commerce has largely ousted Art, and it is not possible to re-convert valuable sites to the ancient purposes of the Buddhist faith.

The Anuradhapura Hotel is beautifully situated in a large garden in the centre of the ancient city. In the tourist season, indeed at most seasons, there is such a rush that a wise traveller books rooms ahead, "lest there be no room in the Inn." Excellent accommodation is provided and every facility is afforded and information given about visiting the ruins. The Proprietor-Lessee is a famous game-shot and authority on sport, and splendid snipe-shooting is to be had all round. In the menu game often figures, and you taste jungle-fowl, teal, or snipe. Elephant chops are a rare delicacy, though this form of nourishment long ago was provided by a gourmand Governor.

CHAPTER VIII

ADAM'S PEKE

IN the interesting map of the Kingdom of Candy Uda in Knox's Ceylon, you will see "Adam's Peke" marked plainly in this pleasant form of spelling by an English printer. He says :—

"On the South side of *Conde Uda* is a hill, supposed to be the highest in this Island, called in the Chingulay language Hamalell; but the Portuguez and the European Nations, Adam's Peak. It is sharp like a Sugar-loaf, and on the top a flat stone with the print of a foot like a man's on it, but far bigger, being about two feet long. The people of this Island count it meritorious to go and worship this impression: and generally about their New Year, they, men, women, and children, go up this vast and high mountain to worship."

Later on, in treating of religion, gods, temples, and priests, Knox wrote :—

"There is another great God, whom they call Buddou, unto whom salvation of souls belongs. Him they believe once to have come upon the earth, and when he was here, that he did usually sit under a large shady tree, called Bogahah. Which trees ever since were accounted holy, and under which with great solemnities they do to this day celebrate the ceremonies of his worship. He departed from the earth from the top of the highest mountain on the Island, called Pice Adam: where there is an impression like a foot, which, they say, is his." Ibn Batuta, an Arab traveller, visited the Peak (which, obviously, Knox never did) about 1350 A.D. and pilgrims of almost every nation of East and West in myriads have visited it since. Mohammedans, both Sunnis and Shiyas, revere it as "The Hill of our Father Adam." Eastern Christians claim the footprint as that of St. Thomas, who, according to early tradition, first preached Christ in South India, and was martyred about the year A.D. 75 at Meliapuram, near modern Madras. To Buddhists the Peak is Sri-Pada, the *Holy Footprint*. To Hindus it is *Siven-oli-padam*.

At the top (which is about the size of a tennis court) is a simple little open Shrine, with a tiled roof set on low pillars, inside which is the sacred Imprint about 6 or 7 feet long. No wonder the High Priest of Adam's Peak is a Prince among Buddhist Prelates! In olden times to climb the Peak was a feat requiring strength and endurance. In the *Journal of a Tour in Ceylon,* 1825, Mrs. Heber, wife of the hymnologist Bishop writes, under date September 15th :—

"From this part of the Candy Road, Adam's Peak, lying to the East, is visible; it is the highest mountain in Ceylon, about 8,000 feet above the level of the sea, and has seldom been ascended, not so much from its height as from the difficulty of the latter part of the ascent, which is quite perpendicular : two ladies, however, have been among the few adventurers, and got up by means of chains and pulleys. The Mussulmans have a tradition that Adam, when driven out of Paradise, alighted upon the Peak, and a mark which bears a resemblance to a human foot is supposed to be the impression made by him, while expiating his crime, by standing on one foot till his sins were forgiven." The Peak is, by the way, 7,420 feet. Pedro, above Nuwara Eliya, is the highest point, 8,290 feet, in Ceylon.

The journal of this literary lady is well worth reading, especially when she says (after describing boa constrictors and alligators):

"The flying leech, which I never heard of before, is very common in the jungles of the interior, and the native troops, on their march to Candy, suffered very severely from their bites. . . . . The smaller ones are very minute; they possess the power of springing by means of a filament, to a considerable distance."

Tired travellers may be relieved to hear that no one has ever heard of a "flying leech" since : but many elephants, the road-makers of the jungle, frequent the forests round the Peak, as do butterflies — Nature's Heavy and Light Brigades, respectively.

A trip to the Peak in these days is a pleasant and not too fatiguing experience. At Hatton, less than 20 miles from the Peak, you can stay in great comfort at the Adam's Peak Hotel, which, after a fire, has recently been entirely re-built in modern style. The Hotel managed by Brown & Co. of Colombo is delightfully situated just above the railway station, and well worth a visit. It is comfortable and well-furnished, and modern throughout. Every facility is furnished for a trip to the Peak. There is an excellent road from Hatton to Maskeliya, and you reach the foot of the Peak after a very lovely drive of some 14 miles. From the top of the Maskeliya Gap you see the Peak, looming to the South in great grandeur. Perhaps one of the best sights in Ceylon is to watch thousands of white-robed pilgrims, young and old of many nations, marching to worship the sacred Footprint. As they go, they often sing. At night they light their little lanterns, and become a chain, as it were, of giant human fire-flies, winding their way along the highways, and then up the narrow by-ways of the Holy Mountain.

As Isaiah has written : *"Ye shall have a song as in the night when a hallowed feast is kept; and gladness of heart, as when one goeth with a pipe to come into the Mountain of God, the Rock of his people."*

It is interesting to note that on the rock wall of the cave named Bhagavalena, about a hundred feet below the summit of Adam's Peak, a Sinhalese King, Nisanka-Malle (1187-1196 A.D.) caused an inscription to be cut when he visited the Peak (*Samanola*) and endowed the shrine.

Close by, a pious Muslim pilgrim carved an inscription in the 12th Century, of which the words decipherable are :—

Muhammad, may God bless him, the Father of Mankind

Saman or Sumana (the Yellow God), whose emblems are a golden bow and arrow, was a mountain deity in Ceylon, the seat of his worship being Adam's Peak, called Sumanakuta in the histories. It is clear that the early annalists believed him to be settled on it before the first visit of Buddha, since it is stated that on that occasion he asked Buddha for 'something worthy of worship', and received some of 'his pure blue (black) locks,' which he enclosed in the emerald dagaba at Mahiyangana.

The best description about the ascent of Adam's Peak is that written by Henry Marshall who accompanied Mr. Sawers, the Commissioner of Revenue in the Kandyan Provinces in 1819.

This account is often copied without acknowledgement. His account of sunrise is worth quoting:—

> "For some time before sunrise, the sky towards the East had a bright flame colour, indicative of the approach of day; and as there were no clouds above us, the sun burst forth suddenly in all his glory, the shadow of the mountain extending, at the same time, apparently for fifty or sixty miles towards the west. In proportion as the sun rose in the sky, light and floating vapours began to ascend from the upper surface of the clouds, and the whole mass below soon seemed to be in a state of transition and rapid motion. Here, however, our observations terminated, having at half-past six o'clock left the summit to commence our descent of the mountain."

The old method of approach from the Ratnapura side was a hair-raising one — by means of chains hung down loosely, and apt therefore to swing giddily in the wind. My old friend Mr. G. B. Leechman of Colombo once bravely ascended in this acrobatic fashion in the 'fifties; but I confess that to me, after hearing his thrilling adventures, this method of ascent was not alluring. Few people, I imagine, still climb up from the South, unless compelled.

So I would exhort you to make this wonderful trip, and join the chosen band of happy Peak-climbers. Climb up the wind-swept path in the evening: sleep till a little before 4 a.m. and then arise, ascend to the summit, and behold the miracle of Dawn, with the shadow of the Peak projected. A well-known Ceylon Scout, Mr. Carl Cook, has described the scene thus:—

"The sun rises, painting the sky with a million colours and rivals only the Aurora Borealis. It is a wonderful sight, this dream heaven. As soon as the golden orb appears, and we have drunk our fill of God's creation, we rush to the parapet wall on the opposite side and there in a dark outline, a perfect cone, its apex touching the vaulted heaven on the distant horizon, lies the famous shadow, now and then flickering the colours of the rainbow at the top and all along its sides, which tradition says is due to the fact that the rays of the sun are refracted through the crystal covering of the venerated Footprint, placed there by God Saman to protect it; which gradually becomes smaller and smaller, as the sun rides higher and higher, until its top vanishes almost at our feet."

Thus you will be granted, perhaps, a mystic vision of the *High and Holy One that inhabiteth Eternity,* with the shadow of God imprinted on cloudland below.

Kaswiri and other Arabian geographers state that diamonds are found on Adam's Peak. This is erroneous. The wealth of The Peak is spiritual, not material. Lately I have studied this Mountain in many aspects when taking colour-films; at early dawn; throughout the day; at sunset. My prevailing impression is unity in diversity — unchanging, as The Mount of Aspiration. Soon I hope to ascend it with other pilgrims, and capture in colour the early-rising rosy-fingered Daughter of Dawn, and the farewell flush of Sunset. For these signify the daily Advent and Passing-Beyond of God, reminding us —

God made us.

God loves us.

God keeps us.

It is no wonder that by religious tradition in Ceylon Adam's Peak is *"only forty miles from Heaven."*

So God is very near.

CHAPTER IX

KANDY TO BATTICALOA AND 'TRINCO

FROM Kandy to Nuwara Eliya — which means Royal Plains — is a pretty run of 48 miles. The best part is the climb up the steep Rambodde Pass. Nuwara Eliya to Europeans is the most home-like bit of Ceylon, being 6,240 feet up. Sir Samuel Baker describes the climate as "Italian" — whatever that may mean exactly! — and records that the opening up of Nuwara Eliya is really due to Sir Edward Barnes, who built the road to it. From Nuwara Eliya the road runs down to Uva through the Badulla gap, anciently known as *"The Path of a Thousand Princes."* While close by in *"The Valley of Rubies"* tradition says stones of great price were found. On the Moon Plains there are signs of old workings, which occasionally lure passengers to prospect for moonstones. Leopards in Nuwara Eliya are a further attraction, but elephants are rarely seen nearer than Ambawela. Beautiful golf links and excellent trout-fishing at an altitude of 6,000 feet with the usual forms of other sport enable each one to pursue his or her fancy. And if it should be a case of two who would be just alone together, the hills all round Nuwara Eliya offer suitable spots for meditation.

Nuwara Eliya is hotelfully supplied. To many strangers within our gates various Clubs extend their privileges. If you wish to stay very comfortably at a hotel, The Grand Hotel at Nuwara Eliya is beautifully situated on a hill overlooking the Golf-Course and the Lake. It is thoroughly modern, very commodious, and the charges are reasonable. The Hotel is a splendid centre from which to see the best that Nuwara Eliya has to offer, and every facility is provided for travellers who wish to watch racing and polo; play golf; go trout fishing; or explore the glorious country around by car. To sit out in the extensive grounds is a delightful form of relaxation and refreshment in the sunshine.

During the season, from Christmas to May, this hill station offers two great joys — golf, and trout fishing — and many attractions — racing, horse-shows, dog-shows and flower-shows. The "little season" in September is quite delightful like a fine

English autumn. The Championship Tennis Meet on excellent hard courts takes place at Easter, and competitors of merit come from far and near to take part. Every year Nuwara Eliya offers new and more attractions; and many more people from India will probably spend their leave in Ceylon when there is a regular flying service *via* Madras and Colombo. I know various hill-stations in India, but I have not found one that combines so many forms of sport and exercise in one as Nuwara Eliya does. Best of all, prices are moderate, and accommodation is ample and good.

The Nuwara Eliya Golf Course is beautifully situated in the long valley below Pedro — the highest point in Ceylon, 8,290 feet above sea level. This is a pleasant mountain to climb, and on a clear day a magnificent view is to be seen from the top. Hunting sambhur with hounds in the forests round Pedro is one of the attractions to sportsmen. The golf-links has plenty of natural hazards, with large excellent greens, and much variety in the natural lie of the land. The course is 6,000 yards in length. Bogie is 74. The longest hole is 576 yards. The trout-stream intersects the course, and you change from club to rod with ease.

Inside the club-house there used to be one feature of great psychological interest. It was a printed notice in Tamil, laying down rules of conduct to be observed by caddies. Here then was the whole creed of the Ceylon caddie. I once obtained a copy of this notice, and had a translation of it made for me by a Tamil clerk of understanding, though he was unacquainted with the game. It is headed seriously :—

COMMANDMENTS TO BAG-CARRYING CHILDREN

and it then proceeds to set out the eight golden rules of Ceylon caddie conduct.

The first commandment says — *"Keep close to Master."* What perfection of counsel in four pithy words! No lagging behind to chat with Perumal; no tarrying near Cargills' shop for a bit of Bazaar gossip; but strict attention to the eminent one, the Lord of the links, Master; you and me, in fact.

In 2 we get the first faint intimation that Master is not always the quite perfect golfer. How well we know it!

"Watch ball," it runs, "if going in river or bush run to help find."

How well we know that river, those gorse bushes that swallow new balls innumerable! Old balls rarely seem to go astray! Once I sliced a drive wickedly high near the General's bungalow. Nobody saw the ball drop. We walked up and looked long — but in vain. An aloe-tree had shot out a long spiky branch at the end of which, twenty feet in the air, was an aloe-blossom, dead but full of seed. Just as we were giving up the search a caddie in a moment of inspiration looked heavenward, and spotted our ball stuck fast in the aloe-blossom. Luckily it was a foursome: but my partner, though the ball was beautifully treed-up, declined to play it. And the caddie sorrowfully picked up — or rather, down.

3 reminds us that the staple industry of Ceylon is agriculture.

"Put back grass where Master cutting." Just like that. And one remembers that the tool of a professional grass-cutter is, for choice, a piece of hoop-iron in Ceylon.

Number 4 refers to audit. *"Count Master's strokes as he playing."*

And so when Master is in some hellish lie the virtuous one in his shrill voice keeps chanting, *"moonoo . . . .nalu . . . . angi . . . ."* — three . . . . four . . . . five, till Master in exasperation contemplates culpable homicide with a niblick under grave provocation.

Number 5 inculcates agility. *"After Master holing in ball hurry for next tee to tee ball."* So that Master's abdominal muscles, already under severe strain from that fatal long drink at the tenth tee (the beer-tree close to the Club-house), may not be further stressed by stooping down.

Number 6 preaches cleanliness. *"Wash Master's ball if dirty."* Some elderly golfers carry an expensive miniature toilet-set in aluminium for the purpose. But the Nuwara Eliya caddie is a child of nature and believes in spit and polish.

Number 7 prescribes a little knowledge. *"Know Bogey to each hole."*

And the wise caddie gives Bogey the benefit of the doubt if Master is a stranger to the course, in hopes of a small *Santosum.*

Finally in number 8 we get a rule of universal application. *"No speaking, not to move, when Master playing at stroke."* Ah! what a comfort to feel that not a flicker of a brown eye-lid, not the tremor of a small big-toe, will mar the accuracy of Master's every stroke. This golden Rule might be generally published on every course in the world.

We hear you asking if these rules are universally obeyed? Could you but see a caddie you would be more than satisfied. A small child, usually smaller than the immense club-bag that he propels, in a blue jersey with N. E. G. C. in red across his skinny chest, with his hair under a nondescript turban or tossing wildly in the breeze, his mud-stained cloth flapping round his diminutive shanks, he is a pathetic little figure in mist or soaking rain. But he has lovely white teeth, a fine spirit, bets heavily on Master's chances, and garners about eight pence a round. After which he is ordered by the caddie-master to "ready up" Master's clubs for to-morrow.

And he possesses the jewel of humour. In his spare time he plays a baby-golf of his own just below the club — each hole a few feet apart. He goes to the caddie school for instruction in letters, grows up — and disappears: as caddying in Ceylon is not yet an employment for those of riper years. With a few exceptions, the lads — usually Sinhalese — play beautiful golf and can lower the colours of some of the best Europeans or Ceylonese. They carry only two clubs — a cleek and a brassie, each much battered but deadly. The secret lies in their putting and in the big-toe grip on the ground. They play boldly for the hole with plenty of cut — and down goes the ball in the most amazing fashion. Given a piping hot summer and fast greens I still hope to see Punchi Singho making a good bid for high honours in England.

Recently in Colombo on the Ladies' Links the Colombo Caddies Championship was played.

In the qualifying round the scores were:—

K. Ebert Perera	...	...	64
J. Sonny	...	...	65
K. D. Sonny Perera	..	...	67
A. Peter	...	...	68

In the Final, the winner returned a score of 57.

And now I come to trout-fishing in Nuwara Eliya — to me, *jam senior,* perhaps the best form of outdoor exercise of all. All fishermen are divisible into two groups — fishmongers, and anglers proper. The former go for what they catch. The latter catch what they go for. But when I see any man of any race with a rod, in tank, by the ocean, or by a stream, I always feel — *"There is a fisherman and a brother."*

I have met fools who say that fishing is no exercise. Well — come and test the truth of that proposition with us in Nuwara Eliya. Leave the Club or your Hotel at grey dawn after a light meal, the grass on the lawn heavy with diamond-dew. Motor out to the Moon Plains, and then on foot, enter the jungle, putting up perhaps an amatory jungle-cock, who indignantly decamps. The *patnas* are still hazy, while thin wisps of mist wind delicately, like a woman's veil, about the dark-blue hill-tops round Pedro. You may see a stag, or put up quail, or flush a late lingering snipe. But to-day they are unheeded. You have other and better game in this, the golden day At your feet through the brown-green velvet of the *patna* runs the silver thread of stream, fringed with reeds and bracken, here in deep pools, there in flashing rapids.

After an hour's walking you reach the Long Pool deep down in the jungle. You pause — take one long deep breath of glorious mountain air; and then begin. The great moment of the year is at hand, when you make your first cast. The fly is an Ogden's Invicta. The date is May 1st. The season ends on October 31st.

Fishing has one great charm, which for want of a better word, I will call the charm of reflection under the blue sky. To the busy brain-worker, the man with many worries, the business-man with a problem to solve, fishing gives the best opportunities for relief. In a city you have the rush and strain of tube, tram, taxi, and telephone. You are like a man sick of a fever. Only in the deep dark-green shade of the forest, or out beside a rippling trout-stream, can you think a matter out clearly. For then your life runs quietly, as God ever meant it to run; with the sun to give you light, clear water to drink, and a bed of sweet bracken to lie down upon and rest. *"God made the country. The Devil made the town."*

The old libellous definition lingers:—"*A fisherman is one who goes out early full of hope, and comes home late full of whisky.*" But this hard saying is only true of some fish-mongers. Rather do I like to think of the hypothetical fisherman, upon whom Izaac Walton laid his gentle commands, in the best of all open-air books, *The Compleat Angler*. Some day, perhaps before so very long, you will come and spend a day with me fishing on the Bo-pats or down the Bul-ela. Our party will consist of 3 — you, myself and Izaac Walton.

If you are wise you will try to meet Abdul, the watcher of the Nuwara Eliya stream. He is a maker of flies that you can buy at Miller's shop — and good flies they are. Better still he knows just where the big fish lie. Three fishermen in Nuwara Eliya require at least four satellites, of whom the breakfast-bearer is most important.

The Long Pool is a natural lake several hundred yards long. At the end is a fine waterfall. We fish till one o'clock. Sixteen fish between the three of us, the best a two-pounder, fill our creels nicely. Then, sleep, lulled to rest by the faint roar of distant falling water.

About 2-30 we wake up again — and so do the trout. We start up-stream, fishing homewards. We have about four miles of beautiful water — deep pools, dark placid stretches, and flashing foamy rapids, fringed by dense jungle, in which a narrow path has been cut down by the edge of the water. Finally, we come to the end of the jungle where the stream winds through the *patna* land. Here are clumps of white arum lilies, and patches of orange mombresia, washed down in flood-time from some estate garden. Glorious dragonflies flit about, and often sit in friendly fashion on your rod. The long shadows cast by Pedro are now falling, and the hills put on marvellous tints of light-green, brown, orange, purple, and gold. A cup of hot tea is refreshing, and we prepare for the evening rise.

And so, in twilight we come to the tea fields of Pedro Estate; put up our rods; and climb the hill to where the car is waiting for us below Pedro factory. Then darkness drops like a curtain, and explains why no fishing is allowed after 7 p.m. Many a joyous day like that do I treasure in my memory. Is such a day lacking in magnificent exercise?

Six and forty more trout-streams, not far away, can be fished by you; but I love the Bul-ela best. In the Hill Club you can see casts of monster trout up to some 16 pounds weight. *"There were giants in the land in those days,"* says Genesis. So was it with Ceylon, when trout were first introduced and food was over-plentiful. To-day a four-pounder is rare. My best so far in this 1937 season was a 2½ pounder. caught in the Bul-ela.

If you have the time, go up to the Horton Plains for two days of trout-fishing, staying at the excellent Rest-house. You can go to Ohiya Station and walk up for three miles; or you can go to the top of the Agrapatna district, and walk about four miles from there. The scenery is like the wilds of Scotland — glorious. While, on your way by road, you pass various excellent trout streams in Dimbula, and the Gorge Valley, containing big fish. You will see many rich tea estates and meet many fine planters, whose hospitality is proverbial.

From Nuwara Eliya to Batticaloa is about 150 miles. We drop down the Hakgalla Pass, visiting the Botanical Gardens on the way, and then come to the Welimada patnas. From Welimada (where the Rest-house is quite a nice one) the road turns off to Bandarawela, but we keep on to Badulla, the Capital of the province of Uva, with a delightful climate and the Highlands all round. We rise up to Passara amid fine scenery.

From Nuwara Eliya, if you can spare a day, I suggest you should make a tour through the lovely Province of Uva, with its highlands and lowlands. Go down the Hakgalla Pass, stopping for an hour at the Botanical Gardens under the guidance, if possible, of courteous and capable Mr. Nock, — worthy son of a worthy father. Then drop down steeply to the wind-blown patnas of Welimada, and climb up and down, and down and up, to Badulla after 37 miles of wonderful scenery. Here you will find a commodious Rest-house, and, close by, a very fine waterfall. After breakfast climb up to Passara, and turn to the right and rise to Namunukula. Then go to Ella and sit on the verandah of the little Rest-house and look down on an immense view that only ends with the sea. In the distance to the East there is a sea of green jungle, *"where there are more bears than men."* From Ella go on to Bandarawela, where there is an excellent yet not expensive Hotel managed by Miller's of Colombo.

It is delightfully situated, modern, and most comfortable. The climate here is delicious, and the air refreshing. I once stayed in this Hotel after an illness, and soon picked up health and strength again. There are many diversions to be had, and the Naval Hill-Station, Diyatalawa (once a Boer-Prisoners' Camp) is not far away. From here through Haputale is a fine road down to Ratnapura — where you are only 50 miles from Colombo. I once cycled this 80 miles on a very wet day.

Now, let us return to our Batticaloa trip, from Passara. On this road started the first motor-mail service of steam-cars run by Mr. Stanley Green. Unhappily steam-cars about the year 1901 were delicate machines which soon broke down on the rough roads of those days: so Mr. Green had to close down, to the general regret of all, save bullock-cart drivers.

From Passara to Lunugala runs a winding road, and then, after passing Lunugala (with another good Rest-house) we drop rapidly through Bibile to a vast expanse of wild country, where animals quite outnumber human beings. I did this trip twice, slowly, by bullock-coach; later I did it twice by car. The road is a very beautiful one, with myriads of birds and butterflies, fringed with thick jungle on each side of the road. At Maha Oya is a fair Rest-house. Butterflies, by the way, migrate 3 or 4 days before the snipe in the first light airs of the monsoon, to assist their flight across the Bay of Bengal. The snipe, which arrive from Burmah and India in October leave on the night of the first full moon after the setting in of the South-West Monsoon — in May or June.

Batticaloa, the Capital of the Eastern Province, is a quiet town of great charm.

On March 29, 1602 the Dutch Admiral Spilberger anchored off Batticaloa, and captured it. The fort was actually built by Noronha, the Portuguese Captain-General. The Dutch yielded it later. In 1639 Batticaloa was again attacked by the Dutch Admiral Westerwold, with an army of 600 men and 6 guns, and captured. In 1659 Captain Knox, his son, and several of the crew of *The Ann* frigate, were captured by Kandyans near Batticaloa. Knox and one other escaped in 1679, reaching Aripo on the western coast on October 15th. They were kindly received at Colombo by the Dutch Governor, Wyklof van Goens.

At Batticaloa there is good snipe shooting and fishing in the lagoons, where the fish are often speared by local experts. Batticaloa is famous for its so-called "Singing Fish" — though science has not yet solved the problem as to which fish exactly causes this euphonious phenomenon. The noise has been described as *"a blend between the croak of a bullfrog and a 'Jew's harp'."* I have heard it distinctly on a full-moon night from a boat on the lake near Kalmunai. It is hard to describe the sound, which is a kind of muffled "honk, honk" deep down in the water, as though a submarine motorist was blowing his conch horn. It is most distinctly heard by holding an oar vertically in the water, and listening at the end of the oar-handle. I can never forget that sail we had that night on the Batticaloa lake in glorious moonlight on a weird craft, while a man and a boy sang, to the rhythmical accompaniment of a tom-tom and small cymbals.

From Batticaloa you can go up to Trincomalee by road and ferry boat. It is not always possible to do this with comfort. I am fortunate in having a description of this road from the well-informed pen of Mr. F. C. Gibbs of Colombo :—

"Trincomalee lies only 75 miles north of Batticaloa ; and one should take this most delightful drive. Almost midway — near Muttur, a little off the road — stands *The White Man's Tree;* so named, because Robert Knox and his men were taken prisoners there in the Seventeenth Century, and carried to Kandy. The road is subject to flooding in the monsoon season, and care should be taken to ascertain whether the road is clear before starting. Apart from about a dozen splendidly-built causeways across minor streams, the car has to be ferried six times across lagoons and rivers, mostly tributaries of the Mahaweli Ganga (*Big Sandy River*). If an early start is made from Trinco, all the ferry-boats are on the right side of the rivers, waiting for the morning mail-bus ; and this saves a lot of waiting — although it may delay the mail somewhat, as the ferrymen's rule is : "First come, first across !"

This trip is somewhat different from others — the intensive cultivation — the vast herds of grazing cattle — the Coast Moors with their quaint straw-plaited Fez hats — and the thousands of wild monkeys, all tend to make it a real Ceylon experience.

Spotted deer walk on the roads in herds — nomad Gipsy tribes can occasionally be seen in encampments by the sea — and at certain times of the year millions of butterflies swarm around the cars, giving a snowfall effect to the surrounding scenery. Although not a bird sanctuary, more varieties of birds can be seen on this road than on any other in Ceylon. Pelicans, storks, and flamingoes are common sights."

Trincomalee, the great Naval Station on the East Coast, has lately changed beyond recognition, from the days when I first knew it long ago as an almost deserted naval station. Its history is interesting, for the possession of such a land-locked harbour was keenly contended for. Indeed, it was one of the keys to India — and still is. Trincomalee's first fort was built by the Portuguese. In 1612 Marcellus de Boschhouder arrived at Kandy and made a treaty with the King. By the treaty the Dutch were permitted to build a fort at Cottiar near Trincomalee. The Portuguese at once destroyed this fort, when built.

In 1639 the Dutch under Admiral Westerwold captured the Trincomalee fort, which was garrisoned with only fifty, who fought well till 23 had been killed. On January 11, 1752, Trincomalee was captured by the English, led by Sir Hector Munro. The naval force was under Admiral Hughes. England was then at war with Holland, and Lord Macartney, Governor of Madras, decided that Ceylon should be conquered. After taking Trincomalee, Admiral Hughes returned to Madras. Taking advantage of this, the French, under the brave Admiral Suffrein, dashed into Trincomalee harbour, and forced the fort to surrender, offering most honourable terms, which were accepted. The Dutch again regained Trincomalee, and held it till on August 23rd, 1795 the English took Fort Frederick after a short siege. Fort Ostenburgh, about 3 miles away, capitulated on August 31. Colombo, as we know already, capitulated on February 15, 1796.

Thus ended the Dutch power in Ceylon.

When the German Crown Prince visited Ceylon a few years before the Great War, he evinced a warm desire to visit Trincomalee yard. His wish was gratified in part. Not a single British soldier or sailor was there: only one old Tamil carpenter, who was mending the Admiral's writing-table! When the party reached a big gate, leading to the top of the hill, the gate was

The Ceylon Tea Propaganda Board

Hindu Kovil in Colombo.

Abhayagiri Dagoba, Anuradhapura

locked, and nobody had the key! The Crown Prince turned to one of his party, and said bitterly, *"Mein Gott! Wenn das doch nur Deutsch wäre!"*

To-day Trincomalee is a hive of industry, being turned into a modern fortress, with a big military aerodrome. The eagles of war have driven out the doves of peace. Trincomalee affords good shooting, lovely bathing, and many residents run down from Colombo and Up-country for pleasant week-ends. There is a railway, now, the journey from Colombo taking some 13 hours. In days of old a visitor to Trincomalee usually stayed at the Rest-House, a long low ancient bungalow, very dark and not too comfortable; but a place where fairly good food was provided by the venerable Rest-House-Keeper named Tamby. He was a splendid old Tamil man; a kind of Elder of the Royal Navy. In his huge red-and-gold turban he looked a fit Host for a Lord High Admiral. To-day there is a new Rest-House. But, far more beautifully situated on a hill overlooking the Harbour, is now The Welcombe Hotel, recently opened. Here you can stay in the greatest comfort, with everything the most exacting traveller can ask for. The food and service are particularly good, and the charges are reasonable. In the motor-boat you can have a delightful cruise of many miles. In fact, if you left the Harbour and steered South, you would not see land till you hit the South Pole. Take my advice and go and stay at the Welcombe Hotel. The sea-bathing is glorious and safe, in blue-green water that is impregnated with sunshine. Trincomalee is now the Spa of Ceylon

From Trincomalee you can go to Colombo through the jungle, by way of Habarana, Dambulla, and Kurnegalle. We will take, instead, the road to Anuradhapura on our way to the Jaffna Peninsula.

Here we enter the Palmyra Paradise. From this amazing tree the Tamils obtain food and oil; palm-wine and sugar; and shade. The matured stem is building-material; the leaves make roofs, rope, fences, mats, hats, and useful baskets, and on them are preserved the Sacred Books of Hinduism. This tree furnishes nearly one-fourth of the means of sustenance of the people of Jaffna. Verily the Palmyra Palm is the Admirable Crichton of the botanical world, only demanding much sand and a little water.

CHAPTER X

OF TREES, HERBS, AND FLOWERS

CEYLON is a land of many beautiful timber-trees, which can be made into excellent furniture. Mr. F. Lewis has written much on the subject and a few notes based on some of his valuable writings may be of interest. Ceylon soil may be classed into five groups which have characteristic properties of their own. They are: (1) Lateritic and lateritious red earth of the Dry Zone. (2) The limestone zone, such as the soil of the patnas and North Matale. (3) The sandy soil. (5) The patna vegetation.

Taken as a whole the soils of Ceylon are poor in organic matter, lime and phosphoric acid, but contain a good deal of nitrogen and potash.

In Colombo the flowering trees are things of glory from March till about July, dominated by the Flamboyants — called the Gold Mohur Tree in India. But most travellers would like to know something of the other trees that line the roads and raise their graceful heads in the jungle.

First comes the Jak, which is found everywhere and is easily recognised by its large green crinkled fruit hanging from the trunk. It yields excellent timber. The nursery rhyme speaks truly of the house that jak built! It is a bright yellow wood, but tones with age to a beautiful dark-brown. The fruit and seeds are extensively eaten, though the former are somewhat glutinous. The wood also supplies the yellow dye for colouring the robes of Buddhist priests.

Ebony is a large handsome tree with broad domed head, dark-grey bark, with many longitudinal black cracks. The leaves, variable in size, are oblong-oval, shining green above, pale below. The flowers are white or yellowish. Just beyond Tangalle Rest-House near the bazaar are several excellent ebony-trees. The wood is very heavy, about 75 pounds per cubic foot. A close relation is Calamander — in colour a pale purplish brown, closely streaked with deep blackish-brown shades of varying intensity. It used to be a favourite wood for drawing-room furniture; but it requires careful handling or it may look very unhappy when used as a cabinet wood. It is the zebra of the timber creation.

Round water one finds the magnificent Kumbuk-tree, which grows to an immense size, with thick pinkish-brown smooth bark.

The Banyan-tree family is common, both in Colombo and elsewhere. The common Banyan-tree drops long arms that take root in the ground. At Kalutara one tree has thus formed an immense arch right across the main road. The familiar Bo-trees, sacred to Buddhists, are common too. Usually a little altar at the foot exhibits the offerings of the devout. All Bo-trees are said to have spread from the historical Bo-tree at Anuradhapura, which is known to have existed from B.C. 288. And another relative is the ill-famed Upas-tree, of which there are specimens at Peradeniya Gardens. Here too are many lovely Amherstias with their masses of flaming pink blossom. Look for them just opposite Peradeniya Rest-House—the loveliest trees of all.

Satinwood is not uncommon. At the last elephant-kraal it was used for the two grand-stands. In olden days the famous one-arch satinwood bridge spanned the river at Peradeniya. It was said not to have a single nail in it — the timbers being simply fitted together with pegs. It is a favourite wood for furniture but is considered by many people to be unlucky. It has the virtue of being white-ant proof.

Kôn is the nearest approach in Ceylon to oak. It is a good hard timber. Some years, ago, by the way, I gave a bit of English oak to my carpenter. He remarked, after using it that it was "*a very nice kind of soft wood*!"

Nedum is another capital wood for furniture. It is heavy and rather brittle when used for chairs, but is most attractive. It grows moderately fast, unlike many Ceylon trees. It is hard to procure in these days, and is said to be found in no other part of the world.

Milla is another fine tree, with yellowish-brown bark and pale-violet flowers, forming small dark-purple fruits. The timber is strong and stands exposure, being largely used for bridge-planks, and oil-casks: while the bark affords an embrocation for rheumatism.

Domba is a smallish-tree with greyish bark and large smooth glossy green leaves. The wood is tough and much used for cart-poles.

Teak has been planted in places by the Forest Department. Some fine trees are noticeable along the road between Colombo and Ja-Ela.

The Katuimbul tree is a beautiful one, tall and shapely, and provides the timber used for matches made in Ceylon.

The Traveller's Palm is an interesting thing containing a good supply of water — hence its dedication to travellers with dry tendencies. The stems of the Korasa-vel also contain large quantities of water. If cut in short lengths and suspended in a vertical position for a few minutes the water pours out steadily. The leaves afford a natural form of sand-paper.

Many trees, like Keku, possess bark that is easily stripped from the trees and made into excellent rope. Much of this I saw used at an Elephant-Kraal. And Lunumidella, owing to its extreme lightness, is used for out-riggers of boats. The plantain-tree by the way possesses juice which is a valuable antidote in cases of snake-bite.

Of the marvellous tree, *cocos nucifera,* no one has ever yet written a full description. From the age of 8 years it starts bearing nuts and enters upon a hundred years of hard labour. Its uses are innumerable. It gives the villager his oil, his nuts, his firewood, and provides all the material for building his home. From it he makes rope, mats, and brooms. In the shape of arrack or toddy it slakes the thirst of the toper or teetotaller. His cattle thrive on the *poonac*, and the surplus of nuts he can always sell for a good price. Lastly, it is the cause of much litigation, criminal and civil, and provides unlimited fees for the legal profession.

Mrs. Heber, in her Journal, noted—

"At present property is sub-divided into the minutest proportions, even to the coconut tree, the 154th part of one of which I have seen advertised for sale."

The tree grows by itself, often unmanured except by accident. And along the sea coast, its slender trunk and graceful branches thrive on a diet of sea-water and sand. It is the Admirable Crichton of the Botanical Universe.

The Tea-bush, one of the camellia tribe, needs no description. The making of tea needs these processes: 1. Plucking leaf. 2. Withering. 3. Rolling. 4. Firing. 5. Sifting. 6. Packing into chests.

Rubber (*Hevea Brasiliensis* grows freely from the sea-level to about 2,500 feet. When the bark is neatly cut, the latex, or milk, flows out. The liquid rubber is congealed in pans by the addition of acetic acid. Next the sheet rubber is smoked to make it keep, and the final product is either smoked sheet or crepe. Roughly speaking, the earning capacity of one acre of rubber is equal to that of two acres of coconuts.

Cinnamon is frequently seen near Colombo, growing in sandy soil in a damp atmosphere. The bush is kept small, and the leaf is rather like that of the laurel. The blossom is white. The cinnamon scent is in the stalk. In 1825 it formed the only considerable export of Ceylon. By the Dutch Law the penalty for wrongfully cutting a branch was the loss of a hand. When Colombo was taken by the British, the value of the stock of cinnamon captured was £186,000. The cinnamon peelers, called Challias, cut the cinnamon branches in lengths of about three feet. They scrape off the bark, and then with a special instrument strip off the inner rind. The cinnamon is tied up in bundles and ready for export. Then you meet it in your puddings.

The iron-wood tree, in the forests of the North-Central Province, bears fruit in profusion, which is eaten by the people, not to mention by bears, deer, and monkeys. In the famine of 1877 this food-supply was of great value. Mr. John Still, by the way, once lost his way with a Governor in the jungle. At last His Excellency became so thirsty that Still had to climb a tree and pick juicy berries for him to eat! Wood-apple pulp acts like chlorodyne; and a certain bean turns muddy water into clean! You rub the inside of an earthen pot with the bean, pour in dirty water, and in a few minutes the sediment sinks, leaving clear water fit to drink. Knox records many herbs and roots of great medicinal value used by the *Vederalas*, or local medicine-men. Indeed the Sinhalese say that every tree has some special benefit for man.

When you return from your tour to Colombo, you should visit the cabinet-making works of Messrs. Don Carolis & Sons in Slave Island, where you will see skilful Sinhalese carpenters using every kind of rare Ceylon timber for furniture. In their spacious premises in Keyzer Street, in the Pettah, this sound old-established Firm of H. Don Carolis & Sons have an immense stock of furniture and fittings to suit every taste and purse.

In Ceylon, names given to lands and gardens in villages are often a marvel to visitors, as trees, hills, gardens, and flowers are charmingly blended. Thus recently in the papers appeared a long list of lands proclaimed under the Waste Lands Ordinances. I take three lands at random — Pahalandaokandealuwatta, 2 acres: Keenagahawilamkumbure, 2 roods: and Jambugahapitiyayewatte, 2½ roods. No wonder the Sinhalese become warmly attached to lands with such attractive names. But in reality the names are simple. Thus Kosgahawatte means just Jak-tree garden. It is like writing your English address in one word: Thelaurelslavenderroadsurbiton. Welsh place-names are more incomprehensible.

In the Government Archives is an interesting book THESAUROS ZEYLANICUS, exhibiting the plants growing in Ceylon, by Joannes Burmann, Amsterdam 1737. The author has made many notes in this copy in M.S. and carelessly left an invitation to a party inside the book, covered with notes. There are capital illustrations throughout this charming book by a very delightful person. All plant-lovers should inspect it. For the rest — for lack of space — I would refer you to Chapter 5 of Knox's Ceylon where he treats:—

"*Of their roots, plants, herbs, flowers.*" I will conclude with his description of "*a flower that serves instead of a dial.*"

"*Its nature is to open about four o'clock in the evening, and so continueth open all night until the morning when it closeth up itself till four o'clock again.*" With this white flower, *Sindrie-mal*, I likewise will close.

CHAPTER XI

TRINCOMALEE TO JAFFNA AND BACK TO COLOMBO

Lo now the High-born Dawn
Shines in the East,
Rousing all men to go forth
To their work and their labour.
The seven yellow Outriders of the Sun
Spur through the encompassing sky.
And the Shining ones
Renew their gift of day.

YOU should leave early, just before dawn, if you wish to see this lovely jungle road at its best. Turn off the main road to Anuradhapura at Horowapatana to the right, breakfasting by the road-side. Close to the road are some hot springs of considerable interest, but not, so far, utilised for healing. Here, traffic is light. You join the Jaffna road at Vavuniya and pass several little rest-houses, at some of which I have stayed. Later you come to Elephant Pass — where at times splendid sport is to be had in catching gigantic mahseer — and enter the Peninsula of Jaffna.

Jaffna is sandy and the soil poor. But the amazing thrift and ceaseless labour of its inhabitants turn even the sandy wilderness into a green garden. The Tamils are called the Scotchmen of Ceylon — a title presumably founded on a certain carefulness in expenditure, and a great pride in pedigrees. But the best parallel is probably to be found in their absorbing love of Education. The schools in Jaffna are well worth a long and careful inspection. After a traveller has wintered in England for a few summers he might well visit Jaffna. For here it only rains for two months in the year. During the other 10 months the sun shines with unclouded fervour. In consequence, Jaffna's climate is well suited for those suffering from lung trouble. The air of Kangesanturai works wonders for consumptives

The fort at Jaffna is a stately fortification in perfect order. The Dutch captured Jaffna from the Portuguese in 1658. Baldaeus, the Dutch Chaplain-Historian, preached a great sermon on the victory. His text was Exodus XVII, 15.

Some people think Jaffna is a little behind the times. Not a bit of it. As long ago as the year 1800, we read that Colonel Barbut, Commandant of Jaffna, and his wife — *"whose engaging qualities exceeded all expectations"* — entertained the Governor, his Chaplain, and his Staff, *"with a degree of luxury and elegance excelled in no corner of the world."*

My own Rest-house experiences in Jaffna have been less luxurious. But I am not a Governor — or even a Chaplain: just a plain chap.

The Dutch Church in Jaffna with its bold outline above the ramparts is a great feature of the Fort. It is no longer in use as a place of regular worship, though it lacks nothing — save a congrégation. Even so, in its solitude, the best time to visit it is on a drowsy Sunday morning. An aged attendant usually emerges from nowhere on the advent of a visitor, and the great door, with a lock of ancient and unoiled construction, reluctantly creaks out permission to enter.

Like the Dutch Churches at Colombo and Galle it is cruciform, and has, to make a guess, seating capacity for some three hundred worshippers. Only a few seats are actually in being at present. The roofed-in prayer pavilion with its satin-wood sounding-board is so positioned that the Preacher could see, and be seen by, everybody. No room here for an attitude of deep meditation and closed eyes, however terrific the heat, for which Jaffna at times is famous! A few box-pews, exhibiting symptoms of senile decay, still cling to the walls. The font in simple purity faces the Western door. On the left is a low gallery, presumably meant for those who made musick: for in front is depicted an elderly black-bearded harpist, probably King David, who gazes at an open scroll with that air of intense admiration that a writer only bestows on his own compositions. To his left frolic two black sheep, while a white one prances upward in search of nourishment from one of those arid and stiff trees, wholly unknown to botanists but beloved by ecclesiastical sculptors. The pulpit is an elegant one with charming proportions, in shape rather like an immense goblet.

It is recorded that the Dutch Governor in Colombo and the two Commandeurs in provincial stations exercised strict authority over the ministers. They even claimed the right of testing the ability of the preacher; and to ensure that his discourse should be a fresh one, and not an old sermon mustily exhumed, they would at times select a text and send it up to the minister after he had ascended the pulpit.

One likes to think of those old-world services of inordinate length, the sermon alone covering upwards of an hour, with the congregation clad in warm good broad-cloth. I recall my own childhood with those two-hour Sunday morning services, (relieved by one bright occasion when I fainted during the Litany and was revived by brandy-and-water as I lay on a convenient tomb-stone near the lych-gate.)

In this church the worthy Dutchman has left his mark with bible and sword. With him foreign service in the East was no light matter. Mr. Anthonisz in his little book already mentioned gives interesting details.

As soon as civil government was established, the Dutch took steps to regulate and order the social condition of the people, whom they placed in the towns and forts which they had conquered. It must be presumed that the ships which brought the earliest settlers from Europe brought chiefly men who were fit to take part in the warlike operations which they had to look forward to in these unsettled regions, and that few, if any, women or children accompanied these pioneers to Ceylon. The absence of Dutch women during these early years appears, however, to have been, in some measure, compensated for by the presence in most of the conquered forts of large numbers of Portuguese women and Portuguese descendants. These the Dutch soldiers were encouraged by the Government to marry, while, in the meantime, the Directors of the Company in Holland lost no time in framing laws and making provision for the emigration of men, women, and children from Europe, who were to populate and colonize the newly acquired dominions. Those who were desirous, either singly or with their wives and children, of going out to Ceylon were accorded passages in the Company's ships free of cost or charge upon their taking the oath of fidelity to the Company. Each person was allowed to carry with him as personal capital no more than 3,000 guilders. Arrived in Ceylon, they were permitted to earn their livelihood by such occupation or industries as they were fitted for, and to carry on any trade, so far as it did not interfere with the Commercial interests of the Company. To those also who wished to take up agriculture as a living, the Company offered free land proportioned in extent to each person's capacity of cultivation. But it was found that, in this respect at least, Ceylon was not a white man's country. The climate and the circumstances were different from those at the Cape, where they had already successfully embarked upon agricultural pursuits. In Ceylon, therefore, the Dutch left these occupations to the peoples of Ceylon, while their own people confined themselves to the towns. Those who came out on the conditions mentioned were not at liberty to return to Europe till 15 years, when the Company's ships were again at their service, on payment of transport charges. The Company's establishment, civil and military, was also, from time to time, increased by the arrival of those who came out on agreements of service, and many of these brought their families with them.

Thus was formed in process of time the Dutch community of Ceylon. It must not be supposed, however, that all those who came out in the service of the Netherlands East India Company were natives of the little Dutch Republic. A very large proportion of the servants of the Company, and many others who settled here, was drawn from the States of Germany, from Denmark, Sweden, France, and even from the British Isles. They came out as subjects of the United Provinces, speaking the Dutch language, and were here all classed together under the one designation — Hollanders or the *"Hollandsche Natie."*

Thus it will be seen that the Dutchman, like his successor the Englishman, went East of set purpose — usually for life, often for death. Accordingly when he left Holland he sometimes took his tombstone as part of his outfit. It was beautifully carved in stone, emblazoned with his arms and his pedigree, with only the date of his death left blank. And the Dutch churches are largely paved with these stern memorials of the past.

Here is one taken at random :—

HIER ONDERLEGT BEGRAVEN
HETLYK, VANDENEHEER
ABRAHAM AARNOUTSZ
VAN BATAVIA, OPPERCOOPMAN

And below in clear beautiful lettering, as fresh as the chisel left it, we read that this worthy was born in 1692 and died 1749. Above his coat-of-arms a peacock is perched in full splendour over what, to a mind unskilled in heraldic lore, look like three gridirons.

An Oppercoopman, by the way, was a Dutch Civil Servant, who drew a Salary of 120 guilders and was addressed as *Wel Edelen Heer*, or Honourable Sir.

One other fragment of those days is to be found in the Bellarmin jugs, which are not uncommon in Ceylon. These vessels are stone jugs with a wide-spreading belly and a narrow neck on the top of which is a rudely-executed face with a long flowing beard. At the back is a handle. The belly in front is decorated with a device or a coat-of-arms of some town in Holland or Germany. The jugs are named after the celebrated Cardinal Robert Bellarmin, who was a conspicuous enemy of the reformed religion. He flourished between 1542 and 1621. Being short of stature and hard-featured, his face and figure were made objects of hatred and derision by the reformers. These jugs will for ever commemorate his inflammatory career. I have picked up 5 different specimens in Ceylon.

In Colombo there is a fine old bit of church-furniture. In a certain church long ago there existed in varying stages of decay a few Dutch seats. Only one was left in decent repair. A certain officer in the Public Works Department noticed this seat and admired it. Whereupon he was importuned by the congregation to present to the Church some new seats! He did so. The church got six bright yellow jak-wood benches. The P.W.D. man got the chair-backed seat. Now it is mine.

You should try and visit Point Pedro, which is a charming little place with an attractive Rest-house facing the sea, about ten miles north.

Jaffna has a charm of her own. As you watch the people at work, your admiration is excited by their untiring industry. A dry and arid land they make into a land of great promise. For every ten gallons of water pumped up, the cultivator gives a gallon of sweat. Such a people must prosper. And Jaffna does.

We return to Colombo along the Jaffna road as far as Anuradhapura, and then take the western road to Puttalam, or the road to Kurnegalle. Puttalam is a town largely inhabited by Ceylon Moors. Not far away is the famous Roman Catholic Church at Madhu, where a great festival takes place in July every year, attended by thousands of devout Catholics. Chilaw, with the remains of an old Dutch fort and a fine old Dutch house on the great sandbank, is a quiet place in the centre of the best coconut district in Ceylon. The Rest-house is well situated by the sea and modern. Next you come down to Negombo — a place of great importance in Dutch times. The big fort (still existing) was taken from the Portuguese by the Dutch in 1640—the same year as Galle fell, likewise. Negombo was taken, a second time, in 1644. Kalutara fell to the Dutch in 1655. In 1646 the Dutch at Negombo carried off some tame elephants belonging to the King of Kandy, who was so enraged that he attacked a body of Dutch troops in the Seven Corles, cut off the head of their Commander, Adrian Van der Stell, and politely sent it in a silk bag to the authorities in Negombo. Later, however, more kindly relations prevailed. Colombo, after a siege by the King of Kandy in alliance with the Dutch, was captured from the Portuguese in 1656, and the King of Kandy, Raja Singha, demanded — without success — that the Dutch should deliver both Colombo and Negombo into his hands. The King claimed the right by treaty. When the Dutch denied his claim, he wrote to the Dutch Captain-General :—

> *"I would have you remember, that such as know not God, and do not keep their word, will one time or another, be sensible of the ill consequences thereof. I know I have God on my side."*

Thus did Negombo make history. To-day it is more famous for fish-tiffins served in a palatial Rest-house, delightfully situated near the sea. When I go there I softly murmur :—

It's an old old failing of our worthy friends The Dutch,
That they want to give too little, and want to get too much.

Incidentally, north of Puttalam, is Mannar, famous for its pearl fisheries. Haughton writes :—

"This famous fishery is of great antiquity; it must have been known in Egypt during the dynasty of the Ptolemies to merchants then trading in the Red Sea and Arabia, if not earlier in Syria to merchants trading in Baghdad and the Persian Gulf. The pearl banks or oyster beds, of which there are a number, are situated on rocky sea-bottom in the Gulf of Mannar, between 8½ degrees and 9 degrees north latitude, sheltered on the west by the coast of India, on the east by the coast of Ceylon, and on the north by Adam's Bridge, the sandy reef stretching between Ramesaram Island and Mannar Island, and are exposed to the open sea only on the south-west, the gulf thus forming a secure place for the development of the oysters and the pearl fishery operations.

The pearl banks cover an extensive area, lying about twelve miles from the coast in water varying in depth from six to nine fathoms. The whole coast for some twenty miles opposite the banks between the Arivi and the Moderagam rivers is more or less strewn with the debris of oyster-shells, many feet deep both above and below the present sea-level, and at the mouth of the Moderagam river, which was the site of a large city in former times, there stand on a cliff over the sea the ruins of a building said to have been occupied by the Kings of Ceylon in those times when superintending the fisheries. A few miles to the south of this cliff lies the conspicuous headland of Kuthereimalai in the Puttalam district, on which Pliny writes that Diodorus Siculus records that a Roman trireme, recovering tribute on the Arabian coast, was wrecked about 200 B.C. having been driven on the Ceylon coast by adverse winds."

Once I bought 2,000 pearl oysters, at a fishery. They arrived in a barrel at my house, "Braemar," in Colombo. I buried the barrel promptly in sand, till the smell had evaporated. From my oysters I got eventually about 64 small pearls. It is all a matter of luck. One small street-boy in Colombo once bought 10 pearl-oysters on spec. In one he found a pearl worth Rs. 400. I might add that you bid for and buy oysters at a Pearl Fishery by lots of 1,000 oysters. The price may vary from Rs. 16 to Rs. 50 per thousand.

I might here mention that a proposal is now on foot to provide a National Park at Wilpattu on the North-West Coast. There is a fine tract of land available, some 212 square miles in extent. The distance from Colombo is about 100 miles. Such a National Park, in which nice clean little huts could be built at suitable spots, (similar to "Jungle-Town" at an Elephant Kraal,) would be a great attraction to both residents and visitors. Most people love hiking and camping, provided it is not too rough and strenuous. In addition, as Wilpattu has a fine sea-board, there would be excellent boating, sailing, and facilities for fishing. It is to be hoped that this excellent scheme will soon come to pass; as Ceylon needs such a Paradise in the north-west for bird and beast, and a new playground for those who love nature study in the wild.

Since the above hope was first expressed, Government, I rejoice to say, has decided to proclaim two areas as National Parks — one at Walpattu, and the other at Yala in the Southern Province. The idea apparently is to create National Land Reserves of approximately 800,000 acres for the preservation of our Flora and Fauna. That reservation, when effected, will mean that roughly one-twentieth of the 16,000,000 acres of land in Ceylon will be dedicated to Nature for ever. Forest Reserves will amount to about 3,000,000 acres more, to assure rainfall and prevent soil-erosion by flooding. The interests of villagers will be protected as regards shooting game for food; but indiscriminate slaughter will, it is hoped, be checked. The trouble is that a hungry man does not respect game laws. And many villagers are extremely hungry.

Minneriya Tank

CHAPTER XII

THE ELEPHANT KRAAL

THREE routes are open to you between Anuradhapura and Colombo. One runs through Kurnegalle to Colombo; the second through Kandy; and the third through Puttalam. If you come through Kurnegalle you will pass through wild country with much jungle, in which great herds of elephants roam. From time to time, by the permission of Government, the Kandyan Chiefs organise what is called an Elephant Kraal. Some years ago I attended such a Kraal near a little village called Galgamuwa; and perhaps some account of what I then saw may be of interest, as such Kraals are only held once in every few years, and tourists have few chances of being present at such an event.

On this occasion for several weeks some thousands of villagers under the leadership of the Kandyan Chiefs in the district had been hard at work rounding up one or more herds of wild elephants. At the end would come the tug-of-war — when, in the presence of privileged spectators, the elephants are driven into the camouflaged stockade. I will try to give a very brief outline of what happens on such an occasion.

The night-mail from Colombo on a glorious starry night with Venus blazing out West — the stop at Galgamuwa Station at the chill hour of 4 a.m. — the Ford car with the usual jumpy head-lights, which bumped as noisily over twelve miles of fear-some dusty jungle-road with steep culverts to Kraal-Town — the temporary "Park Hotel" built of jungle-sticks and cadjans at the dreary hour before dawn — and half-a-mile away to the left a red glare against the pearl-grey sky, that told of a ring of fire within which the herds of wild elephants were detained in uneasy custody: these are a few impressions — and depressions that, slightly blurred, are printed on my memory.

Now and then shots rang out — presently a wild outburst of yells and hoo-cries, made musical by the gentle hand of distance, when an elephant tried to break through — followed by our early-tea in the form of eggs-and-bacon — then the lovely miracle of Dawn. When, as if by consent, hunters and hunted took refuge in silence.

Sunday was over. Another week had begun. It was no day of rest for the elephants.

A walk round the ring of beaters on that Monday morning was extraordinarily interesting. The two herds of wild elephants were confined in a rough square about half-a-mile from the narrow entrance to the stockade. The final drive-in was timed for 9 a.m. next day. All round the cordon, in brilliant hot-weather sunshine, huge fires were blazing — ten to fifteen feet long, giving out intense heat which no elephant would willingly face. A broad path had been cut through the jungle and one saw that man wants but little here below — an axe, a gun, a few jungle sticks and creepers, some *talipot* palm-leaves, a chew of *betel*—and behold! a home from home. Further, a few pots, a bag of rice, a gourd to hold water, some dried fish and vegetables produce a dinner fit for King George himself. And when at five minutes after eleven o'clock the order came, from nowhere apparently, for the line of beaters to advance, without trumpet or even whistle the line rose and advanced in a way that won admiration from a Naval Officer in our party.

That night the scene, along the new line, was weird and beautiful, with the blazing fires, the shouts and yells now rising shrilly, then dying away: the tired figures sleeping in the little huts and amid the pandemonium: and the cheery bands of dancers and singers who made the night gay with rural music and fantastic dances. While here and there, were set up little jungle-altars before which the beaters prayed

"*For those in peril at the Kraal.*"

Of the three drives-in (for the first two attempts failed) I could write much. The excitement was tremendous; the depression, after two failures on Tuesday, acute. But on Wednesday, at seven minutes past eleven exactly, the elephants were driven inside the stockade, and then at last we saw an elephant. Up till then the dense forest had kept them wholly invisible.

We watched the two herds pass through the gate — first one or two — then several in a bunch — then one big fellow at an uneasy trot — then many more. In all 42 elephants were stockaded, including a little one about the size of a large pig. He was a great comedian — a kind of jungle Felix.

I watched the noosing of the wild elephants from a *messa* built of jungle-sticks high up in a tree. The pool of water was just below us, and the thirsty herds at once made for the water. Then after a while they formed up in a solid mass under the trees.

By courtesy *The Ceylon Tea Propaganda Board*

The Kelani Ganga fringed with Beautiful Palms.

Rock Temple—Dambulla.

Presently the attack began, when decoy-elephants and noosers on foot began the work of capture. On sighting the enemy the wild elephants plunged into the pool. Instinct seemed to tell them that massed in the pool they occupied a strong strategic position. But craftily the decoys developed the attack by a flank movement, the great elephant called Beligammana leading them on. Round the edge of the pool they came clearing a path. It was a wonderful sight to see the jungle go flat before them, like corn before the reaper. Great trees crashed down as though made of barley-sugar.

It took time — but gradually the decoys dispersed the herd; and once divided up captures were soon made. About six elephants were secured that evening after many an exciting moment. It seemed to me entirely due to that great beast Beli, who was the King of the Kraal. His history is well known — several lives have been taken by him in his mad moments: but on this day he was really great. He seemed endued with moral power. Once he tackled a wild elephant, it was soon over. His great size, coupled with relative gentleness, his great moral ascendancy impressed everybody: and a big tusker called Kadira supported him splendidly.

The cleverness and agility of the noosers on foot astonished me. Often they were in tight corners, but with the help of a tame elephant or a tree found a miraculous way of escape.

Towards dusk the illusion deepened. All round the outside of the stout stockade the beaters had camped. Inside the stockade a line of great fires sprang up, the òrange flames leaping up against the sombre jungle, while wreaths of rising smoke made a soft haze.

Suddenly a big she-elephant tried to charge the stockade — but long spears and blank cartridges drove her back.

After that — peace.

It only remained to take out the captured elephants before night. The rest of the herd were massed sullenly to our left, looking as though they would yet make one despairing dash for liberty.

But Beligammana stood over against them, like a great rock which the ocean attacks in vain.

The captured elephants were evacuated slowly, but quietly, resisting very little. They seemed to know their hour had come. They went out — almost willingly.

And then came the most moving moment in this vast tragi-comedy of the wild.

It was nearly dark now. The jungle, as in Barrie's *Dear Brutus,* became an enchanted wood, with a foreground of orange, and a back-ground of deep blues and soft greys.

Alone, in his strength, stood the huge black mass of, Beli-gammana, faced by a line of 40 snorting wild elephants, highly enraged.

And then, and only then when his day's work was done and the stockade was cleared of all save himself and his opponents of the morrow, he turned majestically and with unhasting tread marched silently out of the stockade into the night. It was a perfect exit by a mighty beast.

II

If you come along the road to Matale and Kandy, you will pass by the foot of the rocky hill at Dambulla, at the top of which there is an ancient rock temple. It is worth while to stop and examine this temple carefully, as inside it is decorated with vivid paintings of considerable merit, and many images. Parker says :—

"At the side of a flight of steps cut in the rock at Dambulla to facilitate the descent from the celebrated cave-temple, (the largest in Ceylon), to the quarters occupied by the Buddhist monks, near which many other monastic buildings stood in former times, several short inscriptions in colloquial Sinhalese of about the third or fourth Century A.D. were left as records of the commencement of the chiselling work for cutting out the steps. They record the names of pious personages who perhaps bore part of the expense of the work. Such records as *Amataya Wahabaha tani patagati,* (*The place begun by the Minister Wasabha*') and others, leave no doubt as to their general import."

Over a cave at a large boulder lying on the side of the Dambulla hill is another ancient inscription, which reads :—

"The cave of the Thera Dhammarakkhita; given to the Community of the four quarters, present or future. In the reign of Gamani Abhaya it is made."

In this Temple is a wooden statue of King Nissanka Malla, who was born at Sinhapura in India. The statue dates probably from early in the 13th Century and is excellently preserved, being untouched by destruction by white ants.

From Kurnegalle, a picturesque town, surrounded by rocky hills, you have a pleasant run to Colombo through ever-green coconut estates, passing through many prosperous villages.

Most visitors in motors fly past villages.

"Nice village!"
"Wasn't it?"

And miss much. For the village is the real basis of life in Ceylon. In each village there is an officer called the Vidane Aracci. His duties are to collect revenue, suppress or detect crime, and generally run public affairs.

Then there is the Vederala, or country-doctor, with his herbs, roots, and simple surgery. Sometimes there is also a village-dentist—whose weapons would make you shudder, as they are taken out from an ancient bag and used without disinfection. The Kapurala, or Soothsayer, is a mysterious person; and the local Astrologer is universally resorted to for ascertaining auspicious days and hours in all affairs of life. The village *boutiques* (shops) are worth quiet inspection, including the Toddy-Shop or village 'Pub.' The Money-Lender, often an Indian resident, will lend money at low rates—18 to 60 per cent.—and the village "Clever-fellow" will assist you in your litigation. Many villages are torn by factions, each under a Gamarala, or Big Person. In addition there are the Dhobies and Tom-Tom Beaters who assist cheerfully at funerals and weddings. Village life is an interesting study, too often neglected in these days. Someone ought to write a book. "*The Village in the Jungle*" by L. S. Woolf gives a graphic picture, but it refers only to villages in the wild. I should like to see a book on villages in the tame.

CHAPTER XIII

THE WILD MEN OF CEYLON

NOW we will return to the Eastern Province.

Personally, I am no expert in the matter of big-game shooting, though I am keen on snipe for food. Potted snipe on hot toast is a food fit for heroes.

Capella Gallinago (as Linnaeus would have said)
Is a topping little game-bird with a very knowing head:
While Whistler (*vide Index*, under *Fantail, Full, and Jack,*
Or Painted, Pintail) shows him in two shades of brown and black.
The sexes are alike in size, eleven inches long,
Their beaks are built to whistle, but their strong point isn't song.
They spring from marshy herbage with a rapid twisting flight,
And when my gun is ready, well . . . the snipe is out of sight!

I wrote these verses after a happy day of snipe-missing!

If you are keen on big-game shooting you have a wide choice, but perhaps you will find that the village Pottuvil on the East Coast makes a good starting point. You can get there by various roads, (as shown in the map), passing through Wellawaye and Moneragalla. Mr. W. D. L. Perera, a well-known sportsman of Bandarawela, has a charming little shooting lodge there called "Degenham," near the beach in Arugam Bay. In this part of Ceylon are the Resident Sportsmen's Reserve, and the Yala Game Sanctuary, which are accessible from Tissamaharama or Tamanawila. In the latter, beasts and birds abound, and can be studied leisurely. Mr. W. Tutein-Nolthenius, an ardent lover of wild life, recently wrote :—

I have just spent many happy and wonderful hours at the new Bird Sanctuary at the Wirawilla Tank, and the following is typical and true.

A very simple villager came and sat beside me for a yarn, and this is what he said :—

"Is it not splendid that no longer anyone can shoot here? I once did, I shot teal for the Rest-house. Look how the birds have increased, and how they know they are safe," and, with a wide sweep of his bronzed arm, as if a little shy of expressing his feelings he added, "Is not all that beautiful?"

Certainly a teal in the air is worth five in the bag!

At the present time a movement is on foot to create a great National Park, somewhere in this area possibly; but so far nothing has been finally settled. It will be a great attraction to tourists and travellers.

Next, I come to those charming people called Veddahs — the Aborigines of Ceylon. Knox, in his "Contents," puts the matter clearly:—

Concerning the Inhabitants of this Island.
The Several Inhabitants of the Island.
The *Original* of the *Chingulayes*. Wild *Men*.

He describes the Veddahs thus:—

"As in these woods there are Wild Beasts, so wild *Men* also. The land of Binton (*Bintenne*) is all covered with mighty woods, filled with abundance of *Deer*. In this land are many of these wild men; they call them Veddahs, dwelling near no other inhabitants. They speak the *Chingulayes* language. They kill *Deer*, and dry the flesh over the fire, and the people of the Country come and buy it of them. They never till any ground for corn, their Food being only Flesh. They are very expert with their Bows. They have a little Ax, which they stick in by their sides, to cut honey out of hollow Trees. They have no Towns nor Houses, only live by the waters under a Tree, with some boughs cut and laid round about them, to give notice when any wild Beasts come near, which they may hear by their rustling and trampling upon them. They never cut their hair, but tye it up on their Crowns in a bunch. The cloth they use is not broad nor large, scarcely enough to cover their Buttocks. The *wilder* and *tamer* sort of them do both observe a Religion. They have a God peculiar to themselves. The *tamer* do build Temples, the *wild* only bring their sacrifice under Trees, and while it is offering, dance round it, both men and women."

Many writers, like the Seligmanns, have written voluminously about these primitive people and their clans. Unhappily, the Veddahs are sometimes fetched to be interviewed by travellers at a Rest-house, and "assume the rôle of professional primitive man," as Dr. Seligmann puts it.

Gradually the Veddahs are dying out, though a scheme is now being put forward to have a Reservation of Veddah territory, where they could live without interference and hunt to their hearts' content. As a recent German visitor has said:—

"It would be a grave loss to posterity, if through the unrestricted exploitation of the Veddahs by others and through their free contact with external influences, the traces of this primitive species of mankind were lost in the future."

Mr. Parker in his *Ancient Ceylon* gives us an excellent sketch of the history of Veddahs. I only wish I could quote fully from it.

Dr. Spittel, the eminent surgeon of Colombo, is a great authority on Veddahs, camping with them and accurately recording their speech, songs, dances, and ways of life in general. His two books, *Wild Ceylon*, and *Far Off Things*, give such an accurate and interesting description of the Veddahs that I will content myself by referring my readers to them. They can be purchased at Cave's in Colombo. I give a map of the Veddah country by Dr. Spittel's permission. Here are shown the trails that he followed, and which his books describe with such vividness and fascination. John Still is also an authority on the wild folk of our jungles, as you will see in *The Jungle Tide*. Mr. Marett, our anthropological expert, has kindly given me a typical group of Veddahs, taken recently. Enlarged spleens — a common defect—are responsible for the abdominal distention.

At one time people used to slaughter wild animals indiscriminately at night, at water-holes, or by attracting them by projecting beams of light from an electric-torch. One sarcastic writer put this practice plainly thus in a letter to a local paper recently:—

"Don't give an animal half a chance, kill it outright as I have seen it done by torch-light. The experience was such, that I had to warn the killer from going too close lest the animal ran up the barrel and with the bang the brains of the hare met its tail."

The Veddahs to-day are threatened with civilisation. I personally would leave them alone in the jungles they love so dearly.

A little evening hymn, written long ago, prays for protection for Forest Folk in the night.

In You, O Gods, we safely rest,
Like men in coats of armour dressed.
May dangers pass our small abodes,
As charioteers avoid rough roads.
Lead us to pleasant paths abroad,
Like horses to a shallow ford.
Protect all Beings and all Things,
As birds extend their sheltering wings.

CHAPTER XIV

ANURADHAPURA AND MIHINTALE

THE great Buddhist Chronicle called *The Mahavansa*, covering roughly the period B.C. 500 to A.D. 300 (available in an English translation) is the mine of Sinhalese history in which all writers dig. It is a picturesque, dramatic, priestly narrative of great interest; and travellers would be wise to buy a translation of the book and study it before and after, visiting Ceylon. Father Perera, S.J., has written lately :—

"The year 1937 is the Centenary of the first publication of the translation of *The Mahavansa* by George Turnour. We are now so familiar with the name and significance and authority of the great Pali chronicle, and we have so many editions and translations of the work into English and Sinhalese, that we can scarcely realise the epoch-making character of Turnour's work. It was he who first vindicated the authenticity of the chronicle and it was his publication that established its reputation for good. Before his day it was of course known that there was a chronicle called *The Mahavansa*; but it was known but vaguely and was looked upon as a mere collection of legend and fable, a sort of religio-mythical *purana*, scarcely worth the serious attention of historians. The reason for this misleading view was the great neglect into which the chronicle and Pali studies had fallen in the very country which was the subject of the chronicle. Not more than two copies were even known to exist at the time. Even sixty years later, when Geiger was preparing his critical text, the chief manuscripts that he consulted were two copies in the Burmese character brought from Mandalay.

It had never been translated into Sinhalese. There was a general belief among the *literati* that a commentary of *The Mahavansa* had been in existence, though not even the most learned had ever seen it, till the investigations of Turnour succeeded in tracing one in the Mulgirigala Vihara in 1827. *The Mahavansa* strictly so-called is the epic poem of Mahanama. It was continued by Dharmakirti, according to tradition, at Anuradhapura under Parakrama Bahu the Great; Tibbotuwe at Kandy under Kirtisri; and by other scholars afterwards. The continuation is not *The Mahavansa* properly so-called; though of course the term *Mahavansa* may be used to denote the whole historical compilation, and is sometimes so used in the chronicle itself. Thus *The Mahavansa* is the old chronicle, and the later chronicle is *The Suluvansa.*"

The city of Anuradhapura, the ancient capital, dates from about 410 B.C. and lasted up to A.D. 1109. It was called after a follower of Wijaya, named Anuradha. Later the city was enlarged and re-designed in the reign (308-275 B.C.) of King Pandukabhaya; and in *The Mahavansa* it is described as nearly 16 miles square at the height of its prosperity. The population was large, judging by the tales of writers of old. I think perhaps it will be best to take as our guide and friend here the celestial Monk, Lung, who spent two years in Ceylon, A.D. 411. He wrote a long and learned treatise, of which Chapter 38 deals with Ceylon. He was a Chinese Buddhist Monk, who, "*wishing to be far from the dust and vulgar ways of life, chose monkhood.*" He took the pen-name of Fâ-Hien, meaning "*Illustrious Master of the Law.*" Hence he makes a natural appeal to a lawyer! He writes:—

"The country originally had no human inhabitants and was occupied by Spirits and *Nagas*, with which merchants of various countries carried on a trade. When the trafficking was taking place, the spirits did not show themselves. They simply set forth their precious commodities, with labels of the price attached to them; while the merchants made their purchases according to the price, and took the things away. Through the coming and going of merchants in this way, when they went away, the people of their various countries heard how pleasant the land was; and flocked to it in numbers, until it became a great nation. The climate is temperate and attractive without any difference of summer or winter. The vegetation is always luxuriant. Cultivation proceeds whenever men think fit; there are no special seasons for it."

Later he describes the advent of the Buddhist faith to Ceylon:—

"When Buddha came to this country wishing to transform the wicked Nagas by his supernatural power, He planted one foot at the North of the Royal City and the other on the top of a mountain, the two being fifteen *yojanas* apart. Over the footprint at the North of the City, the King built a large tope (*Cantonese, T'ap*) 400 cubits high, grandly adorned with gold and silver, and finished with a combination of all the precious substances. By the side of the *tope* (*i.e., Dagaba*) he further built a monastery called the Abhayagiri, where there are now 5,000 monks. There is in it a Hall of Buddha, adorned with carved and inlaid work of gold and silver and rich in the seven precious substances, in which there is an image of Buddha in green jade more than 20 cubits in height glittering all over with these substances, and having the appearance of solemn dignity which words cannot express. In the palm of the right hand there rests a priceless pearl."

Of the sacred Bo-tree, brought from Buddha Gaya in North India, he writes:—

"A former King of the country had sent to Central India and obtained a strip of the Patna Tree, which he planted by the side of the hall of Buddha where the tree grew up to the heights of 200 cubits. As it bent on one side towards the South-East the King, fearing that it would fall, propped it up with a post eight or nine spans round. The tree began to grow at the very heart of the prop where it met the trunk; a shoot pierced through the post and went down to the ground, where it entered and found roots that rose to the surface, and were about four spans round. Although the post was split in the middle, the outer portions of the shoot grew, and people did not remove them. Beneath the tree there has been built a Vihare, in which there is an image of Buddha seated, which the monks and commonalty reverence and look up to without ever becoming wearied. In the city there has been reared also the Vihare of Buddha's tooth, on which, as well as on the other, the seven precious substances have been employed."

As regards the people of the City he writes:—

"In the city there are many Vaisya elders and Sabaean merchants, whose houses are stately and beautiful. The lanes and passages are kept in good order. At the heads of the four main streets there have been built preaching-halls where, on the 8th, 14th, and 15th days of the month, they spread carpets and set up a pulpit; while the monks and commonalty from all quarters come together to hear the Law. The people say that in the kingdom there be altogether 60,000 monks who get their food from the common stores. The King besides prepares elsewhere in the city a common supply of food for five or six thousand more. When any want food, they take their begging-bowls and go to the place of distribution, and take as much as the vessels will hold, all returning with them full."

I like one little episode recorded by Fâ-Hien. He listened to a lovely little sermon preached by an Indian devotee on Buddha's Alms-Bowl. The Preacher foretold one day The Return of Buddha.

Fâ-Hien wished to write down the preachment as a portion of inspired doctrine; but the man declined, saying, — "This is taken from no Holy Book. It is just the utterance of my own mind."

Few modern preachers would be equally modest.

The Festival of the Exposition of the Sacred Tooth is vividly described: "The tooth of Buddha is always brought forth in the middle of the third month. Ten days beforehand, the King grandly caparisons a large elephant, on which he mounts a man who can speak distinctly, and is dressed in royal robes and commanded to beat a large drum, and make the proclamation following:—

"The Bodhisattva, during three Asankhyeya-Kalpas, manifested his activity and did not spare his own life.... He gave up kingdom, city, wife, and son; he plucked out his eyes and gave them to another; he cut off a piece of his flesh to ransom the life of a dove; he cut off his head and gave it as alms; he gave his body to feed a starving tigress; he grudges not his marrow and his brains. In many such ways as these did he undergo pain for the sake of all living. And thus it came to pass that having become Buddha, he continued in the world for 45 years preaching his law, teaching and transforming all, so that those who had no rest found rest, and sinners were converted. When his connection with the living was completed, he attained Pari-Nirvana and died. Since that event, for 1,497 years, the light of the world has gone out, and all living beings have long continued in grief. Behold! Ten days hence the Buddha's Tooth will be brought forth, and taken to the Abhayagiri Vihare! Let all on earth. whether monks or laics, who wish to win merit, make the roads smooth; nobly adorn the highways and byeways; and provide abundant store of flowers and incense to be used as offerings."

Flowers always play a great part in ceremonial in the East. Sometimes you will meet on a *poya* night a *Mal Perahera*, or Flowering Procession, going to the temple. In front, in single file, come children bearing flowers; behind them walk women dressed in white, bringing their offerings for the priest, with just a few simple lanterns to light them along the village track that leads to some little temple. A *tom-tom* adds dignity and rhythm to their march.

Fâ-Hien, in an earlier chapter, tells us that after the death of Buddha at the city of Kusinara, the eight Kings divided the relics from the burned body. From here came, by tradition, the Sacred Tooth to Ceylon. There are four great *Topes* in India, to recall when Buddha was born; when he attained to Wisdom; when he began to move the wheel of the Law; and when he attained-Nirvana.

On the day appointed for the Tooth-Relic Procession, (as we read in *The Mahavansa*,) lavish decorations made the road a maze of colour, with silken streamers, and fragrant canopies of flowers, as the Relic was borne solemnly along on the back of a huge State-elephant, much as it still is to-day in Kandy in the month of August.

It may surprise visitors to be told that in those early days town-planning was already an exact science. King Pandukabhaya arranged that his Veddah allies should be quartered on three sides of his city, to defend it. He gave them, too, a site for their temple to the Veddah God. He laid out a great cemetery on the western side, (hence, our modern expression, "*Gone West*," for death). He made a great road to Nahatittha, the port from which passengers went to South India. He also laid out splendid flower-gardens near the Kadamba River (now the Malwatte-Oya) and built the city walls, with a great gate facing each of the cardinal points. Part of the garden was "*in a delightful forest, cool from its deep shade and soft green turf.*" There was another greater garden, the Mahamegha, planted with fruit-trees and flowering shrubs. The gardens were under the care of the monks of "The Great Monastery." The entire city was under a Royal Conservator, a nephew of the King. In the larger garden was placed the Sacred Bo-Tree. I quote here from Mr. Edward Perera :—

"The Nuwarawæwa family, seated in the neighbourhood of the Sacred Bo-tree of Anuradhapura, has a unique history. They are the hereditary custodians of the fig-tree, sprung from a shoot of that under which Gautama attained Buddhahood. Among the princes who escorted the shoot from the Court of Asoka the Great (*circa* 257 B.C.), Prince Bodhigupta and his descendants were solemnly entrusted with the service of the plant by King Dewanampiyatissa. Kings and dynasties have passed away, and Anuradhapura itself is but a ruin; yet to this day a member of the family watches over the tree. Sir Emerson Tennent, in 1859, thus refers to a youthful representative of the clan: 'The Chiefship of the district has been ever since in the same family, and the boy, who bears the title of Suriya-Kumara-Singha (Prince of the Lion and the Sun), can boast an unbroken descent, compared with whose antiquity the renowned peerages of Europe are but creations of yesterday.' "

King Pandukabhaya was the greatest organizer of the Kings of Lanka; he defined the boundaries of all villages; astutely enlisted the help of the war-like Veddahs; strengthened the priesthood; and was the first systematically to build tanks, and encourage irrigation. He was called "*The Wise Ruler, whose country was in a state of perfect peace.*" He did all this, after deposing his uncle in 308 B.C. He died in 275 B.C.

The ancient Capital of Lanka was at Upatissa, but King Pandukabhaya transferred the Capital to Anuradhapura about the year 300 B.C. I have taken my dates mainly from Mr. Parker's *Ancient Ceylon*; but I should mention that historians are by no means agreed on many of the dates mentioned.

Now let us go with our celestial friend to Mihintale, where the Buddhist faith, by ancient tradition, was first delivered to Ceylon. Buddhism was first preached by Siddattha Buddha, (who died about the year 485 B.C.) and was originally designed as a purified form of Hinduism. In the reign of the Emperor Asoka, about B.C. 242, according to Sinhalese tradition, the first Buddhist Emperor in India sent his son Mahinda to preach the new faith in Ceylon. The King of Ceylon at that time was Devanampiyatissa — a mighty hunter and a friend of Asoka, who reigned 245-225 B.C. As this King was returning one evening from hunting deer on the slopes of Mihintale, he met the apostle Mahinda; heard from his lips the new message of Buddha; and was converted, with all his household, and many of his subjects. The sacred place of meeting was marked by the Ambasthala Dagaba; built in A.D. 15 by King Mahadathika. This, contrary to others, is built of stone, quarried on the spot: while further up the holy hill another Dagaba enshrines the ashes of Mahinda. The stone couch of Mahinda may also be seen. The festival of Poson, in the month of June, celebrates this great occasion; while the feast of Wesak in the month of May, celebrates the birth of Buddha. Mihintale is a sacred hill for ever, as befits the spiritual womb of Buddhism in Ceylon. Let Fâ-Hien give us his account:—

"Forty *le* to the East of Anuradhapura (= 9 English miles) there is a hill, with a Vihara upon it, called *The Chaitya*, where there may be 2,000 monks. Among them there is a *Sramana* of great virtue named Dharmagupta, honoured by all the Kingdom. He has lived for about forty years in a chamber of stone, showing such gentleness of heart that he has brought snakes and rats to dwell together in the same room without doing one another any harm."

A famous ascetic of Mihintale founded a school which flourished in B.C. 400. So Mihintale is holy ground from very ancient times.

After the first meeting on Mihintale, King Tissa invited Mahinda and his four companions to the Royal Palace in Anuradhapura to expound more fully the doctrine of Buddha. Accordingly, one afternoon, Mahinda preached in the Royal garden, and, led by the Princess Anula, countless women of the first rank resorted thither, and ranged themselves round the *Thera*. (Mahinda). Having bowed down, the ladies made pious offerings, and Mahinda began to teach. He spoke for some hours; for we are told, "*when he exchanged final greetings, night had fallen.*"

Thus did Buddhism replace Brahmanism (or Hinduism) and become the national religion of Ceylon. Here it is worth remembering that while in Greece or Italy the stately ruins of to-day were originally glorious buildings to honour dead faiths, the Buried Cities of Ceylon are testimony to the faith still professed by millions of Sinhalese to-day. Through them Mahinda, though dead, still preacheth.

Knox mentions the fate of Anuradhapura and other cities: and tells us that the King had left the city, and "*it is now quite gone to decay.*" In Knox's time the capital was "*Digligy-Neur towards the East of Cande, lying in the country of Hevahatt.*"

He continues:—

"There are besides them already mentioned, several other Ruinous places that do still retain the name of cities, where

Kings have reigned, though now little Foot-steps remaining of them. At the North end of this King's Dominion is one of these Ruinous Cities called *Anurodgburro*, where they say Ninety Kings have reigned, the spirits of whom they hold now to be Saints in glory, having merited it by making *Pagodas* and Stone Pillars and Images to the honour of their *Gods*, whereof there are many yet remaining: which the *Chingulayes* count very meritorious to worship, and the next way to Heaven."

He then describes some ruins of stone bridges that he saw when escaping, and says, "the Country is all desolate without Inhabitants." He sums up the reasons for the downfall of these cities of old:—

"There are many of them here and there lie desolate, occasioned by their voluntary forsaking them, which they often do, in case many of them fall sick, and two or three die soon after one another: For this they conclude to happen from the hand of the *Devil.* Whereupon they all leave their town and go to another thinking to avoid him: Thus relinquishing both their Houses and Lands too. Yet afterwards, when they think the Devil hath departed the place, some will sometimes come back and reassume their Lands again."

Happily, however, the day is at hand, thanks to modern research, when the words of Isaiah may be applied to this fair portion of Ceylon:—

"Thou shalt no more be termed Forsaken; neither shall thy land any more be called Desolate; but thou shalt be called *My Delight is in her*, and thy land Married; for the Lord delighteth in thee."

One cool evening, long ago, I trod the path with its 1,800 steps, that gently lead one to the top of Mihintale. At the bottom are long stone troughs, in which, ages ago, food was placed for priests, of whom thousands were gathered round the holy Hill.

To-day in England we have the "Friends of Canterbury Cathedral." In those days each Víhara had its "friends," and still often has. Such "friends" gave bricks for buildings, upon which their initials were stamped, as an act of religious merit. They also provided rich endowments.

As you climb Mihintale slowly, pause to look at a small cistern cut in the rock to your right. A great artist has carved out of the living rock above the cistern a magnificent hooded cobra, that looks sinuously alive, though for ever motionless.

I was reminded, as I climbed up, of the twenty-fourth Psalm of the prophet David, which is the hymn of all good climbers. Looking down from the top over the fertile plain below, one sang in spirit:—

"The earth is the Lord's and the fulness thereof."

I wonder if Fâ-Hien knew the Psalms?

Mihintale to-day is arrestingly beautiful: but in a few more years it will be deemed as noble a monument to the Buddha as any the world can show. So give at least one long day to the Holy Hill. You will not regret it: especially if you see it at Sunset.

Then night falls, and, in fantasy, the Goddess appears:—

Night coming on through fading skies,
The Goddess shines with gleaming eyes,
Patterned in flickering fireflies.

Immortal Deity of Night,
She fills the valley, fills the height,
And conquers darkness by her light.

The hamlet sleeps beneath the hill,
The hungry kite at length is still;
But hungering beasts steal forth to kill.

So come to us, dark Goddess blest,
As birds upon their tree to nest,
Beneath thy wings we go to rest.

Let not the were-wolf seal our doom,
Nor robber 'cross our doorway loom,
But bear us safely through the gloom.

And when at last black night is gone,
And giveth place to golden dawn,
Let us awake like those reborn.

CHAPTER XV

CONCERNING POLONNARUWA

I think, perhaps, of all the low-country places I know, I like Polonnaruwa best. It is far from the main road : though to-day the railway has pierced the wild. You drive through glorious wild park-like scenery and (if you are wise) arrange a picnic meal on the banks of Minneriya tank — a lake of peace, especially lovely as evening shadows fall, and Buddha's rays shoot up from the setting sun. Long ago I saw a lonely fisherman, far out in Minneriya tank at sunset, performing the act of faith, whereby one often toils long and takes nothing. I called that picture "Hope." After Minneriya (now a blessed bird-sanctuary) one goes into thick jungle again, which is alive with butterflies, birds, and beasts. And then just at dark perhaps you see great shadowy ruins; you are in Polonnaruwa. The contrast of now and long ago is vividly seen. Was it not said of old — *"A hen may walk from Anuradhapura to Polonnaruwa along the house-tops."*

This city owes more to Tamil influence than Anuradhapura.

Anuradhapura was destroyed early in the 11th Century A.D. by Chola invaders from South India, and the conquerors who were Hindus set up their Capital in Polonnaruwa, and built a stone temple to Siva. King Vijayabahu I, (after his coronation) drove out the Cholas from Polonnaruwa about 1075 A.D. and reigned for 33 years in this city, which thus became the Sinhalese Capital. After various vicissitudes, in the 14th Century, Polonnaruwa was abandoned, and the jungle soon buried the great buildings. The remains of the King's Palace can be seen near the Rest-house. This Palace (stated to have been of seven stories containing a thousand chambers) was obviously a noble building, even allowing for some pardonable exaggeration. The Thuparama, a splendid type of Sinhalese architecture, after some restoration, is practically perfect, and is unique in that it still possesses a roof. Polonnaruwa had five hundred years of greatness — from the 8th to the 13th Century A.D. There is a large Rest-house charmingly situated on a little hill, overlooking Topawewa Tank

VEDDAH COUNTRY
of
EASTERN & UVA PROVINCES
REFERENCE
MAHAWELI GANGA
MAHAOYA TO BIBILE
BINGODA
PROVINCE BOUNDARY
ROADS
CART TRACKS
FOOTPATHS
PUBLISHED BY COURTESY
OF DR R.L.SPITTEL
EASTERN PROVINCE
UVA PROVINCE

Knox's Ceylon

Treading out Rice

constructed by King Upatissa in the 4th Century A.D. I have noticed that fireflies congregate very brilliantly round this peaceful habitation at night.

Rise next morning before dawn, and listen in imagination to an ancient Vedic song: for in those days music and singing were more common than they are in daily life now. One singer led the multitude, thus:—

THE SONG OF THE GOLDEN CHILD

One *In the beginning there arose the Golden Child:*
He was born the Lord
Of all things that are.
He established the goodly Earth
And the star-pierced sky.

All *Who is the God to whom we shall offer our sacrifice?*

One *In the beginning there arose the Golden Child:*
He who gives life, who gives strength,
Whose command the Bright Gods revere;
Whose shadow is immortality,
Whose shadow is death.

All *Who is the God to whom we shall offer our sacrifice?*

One *He through his power is the Lord of All,*
Lord of the fast-awakening world;
He it is who governs all in all,
Both man, and bird, and beast.
Rejoice, rejoice, shout with the morning stars:
The dawn of day is a mirror
Held up for his shining countenance.

All *He is the God to whom we offer our sacrifice.*

The song is compiled from old Vedic sources, and is merely an attempt to recreate the atmosphere of those times.

Polonnaruwa was anciently called Pullattinagara. Most of the present ruins date from the 10th or 11th Centuries. Both Tamil and Sinhalese art and architecture flourished here in turn, and the remains still exist side by side: hence in parts there is a puzzling confusion of styles.

The imposing mass of the Jetawanarama Vihare is the largest Buddhist building, with the Kiri Dagaba close by. These buildings to my mind are particularly beautiful if seen in the bright moonlight, as they form such a satisfying composition from the aesthetic and spiritual point of view. When I first saw these ruins long ago, they were compassed about with more jungle-trees than is the case to-day. Perhaps the Watadage, a circular building, built to contain the Tooth-Relic by King Nissanka Malla (1198-1207 A.D.) with four great silent Buddhas eternally gazing in deepest contemplation, North, South, East, and West, is most impressive aesthetically, for it imports a deep sense of comfort and repose, if you sit and gaze steadfastly at its gracious lines. I like the flights of steps leading up to the Four Enlightened Ones, seated with hands folded and legs crossed, according to the ancient canon of Buddhist ecclesiastical art.

Well have I disciplined myself at last
In thought, in speech, in deed, by concentration.
Desire with all its roots is rooted up :
And calmly I can enter Peace Eternal.

In old, old, Polonnaruwa you can wander far and wide in forest and in glade, always finding new vistas of departed glory — though possibly these ruins are even more moving in decay than they were in their prime of rich decoration in gold, red, and yellow, and other bright colours; of which traces still remain and can be seen, if you search diligently.

There are here, naturally, several Sivite Temples and Shrines erected by Tamil kings, who came over from India and by conquest ruled the Sinhalese at certain periods, and altered buildings dedicated to Buddha. Such buildings originally would have paid honour to Nandi (the stone Bull of South India). But the Sinhalese Kings in turn destroyed many Sivite shrines and emblems, and erected in their place fresh images of Buddha Hence the architectural confusion that is charming, but puzzling, to the layman's eye. Here too recently were dug up many of those striking bronze figures of dancing Nadaraja (Siva) and other Indian deities, that are collected now in the Colombo Museum. What has chiefly changed the Tamil aspect of Polonnaruwa is the mass of buildings erected by two Buddhist King·

fervent devotees of Buddha — King Parakrama Bahu I (in the middle of the 12th Century A.D.) and King Nissanka, who succeeded him. King Parakrama Bahu reigned for thirty and three years, and slept with his fathers. Now the rest of the acts of Parakrama Bahu and all that he did, and the buildings that he made, and the cities that he built, are they not written in the book of the Chronicles of the Kings of Pulattinagara?

I have kept to the last the best thing of all — indeed, to my mind, one of the best things in the whole world. of which I have seen a good deal. In the cool of the evening, walk or drive the short distance to the Gal-Vihare. It stands at the end of a glade. The little shrine is hewn out of the long low mass of living rock, with the huge Buddha sleeping, and the sleepless figure of his disciple Ananda watching, erect at his head . . . . . . It is peace eternal — the most moving, yet most comforting sight in the East that I know. Never has death been so beautifully depicted . . . . . no Terrors here, only rest, infinite, deep, and abiding.

In spirit, I often go back to that lovely little glade, at sunset, the hour of many cooing doves. I would say, (varying an ancient saying) :—

If there is a place of Peace upon Earth,
It is here, it is here, it is here.

I will close this chapter with :—

A Song of the Forest at sunset.

Soft sounds of grazing fill the night,
A little hut looms close beside;
And Aranyani, Forest-Sprite,
Creaks like a cart at eventide.

Here someone calls his herd to him:
Another chops a log hard by:
Who tarries in the forest dim
Thinks to himself, "What was that cry?"

Never does Aranyani kill,
Unless too close one rashly creeps.
When She of fruit has had her fill,
At her sweet will She softly sleeps.

Sweet-scented, redolent of balm,
Replete with food though tilling not,
Mother of beasts, I sing thy charm,
And envy Thee thy woodland lot.

Recently I revisited Polonnaruwa, twice. It is more lovely than ever; as I hope to show in the sequel to this Book, to be called "More about the Real Ceylon."

Here would I rest awhile, and meditate —

Until the day be cool.

And the shadows flee away.

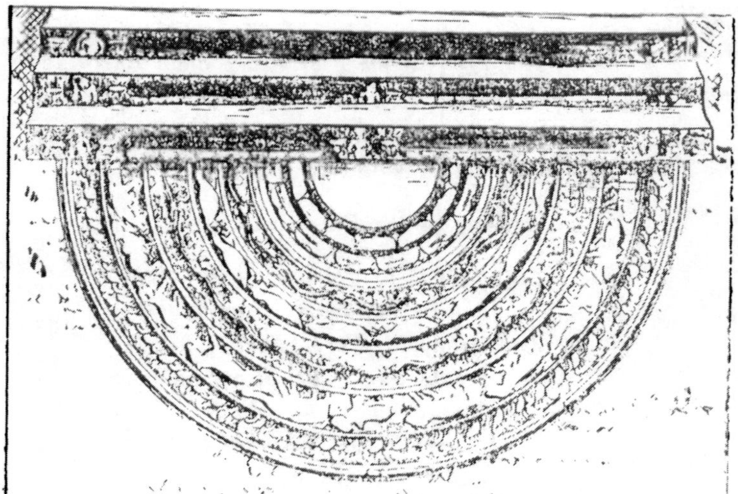

Moonstone at Polonnaruwa.

CHAPTER XVI

THE ROCK FORTRESS OF SIGIRIYA

Now we come to the outstanding feature of the Low-Country of Ceylon — the Hill-fort of Sigiri, set in a frame of jungle, pure and undefiled, about eight miles from the Dambulla-Trincomalee main road. Once we left Colombo at ten o'clock at night for Sigiri. I had had a long day and was tired. But I drove to Dambulla all the way, nearly going to sleep at the wheel in the bright moonlight. Dawn woke me up, and at the turn-off to Sigiri I made a big fire, as it felt chilly; got early tea ready; and did some physical exercises on the road to unstiffen my muscles, after a long drive. Then I awoke the others, who had slept peacefully all night, only waking up for light refreshment at Kurnegalle.

Sigiriya is unique — rising 400 feet sheer from the flat plain, with a touch of yellow or rose-colour in certain lights. Try and visit it when there is a moon. Start after tea, and climb to the top just before sunset. Then come half-way down, while it is still quite light and wait on the plateau below the old Lion Gate for supper. Listen to the jungle below as the birds go to bed, and the beasts of prey go forth to seek their meat from God. Presently, heralded by high lights, you see the golden moon rise. For the moon in Ceylon rises golden, and then turns silvery in the heavens.

Finally descend the hill by the light of a *chulu* — just a palm-leaf-torch. And you may see far down the gallery the lonely spirit of the wicked Kasyappa, who slew his father and turned Sigiriya into a hill of refuge.

The wicked are usually remembered: the good forgotten. Wherefore hearken to the tale of the wicked Kasyappa :—

Somewhere towards the end of the 5th Century of the Christian Era, the Sinhalese King Dhatusena, after years of hard fighting with the Tamils from Southern India, won to victory, and restored the land to peace and prosperity. Though a much married man, he had but one daughter and two sons, of which

Kasyappa was the younger. The daughter married Migara, Chief of the army and nephew to the King through his mother, the King's sister. Quarrels ensued, and Migara beat his wife with so much ardour that blood came. The King, in great wrath, seized Migara's mother, and had her stripped and burnt. Migara then rose in revolt, after persuading Kasyappa to join him, and conquered the country, taking the old king prisoner; while Moggallana, the heir, fled to India. Kasyappa now reigned in his father's stead, but, not content with the throne, spent his time ceaselessly urging the old King (no doubt without much gentleness in the methods used) to reveal his treasures. Wearied by these importunities the King promised to show the principal treasures he had left, if taken to Kalawewa, the great tank that he had constructed during his reign. Here lived an old monk, a friend of his youth; and when the King had bathed in the tank and had drunk from its waters, the two old men sat down and talked of bygone days in this world, and future days in the next. Turning then to Kasyappa's emissaries, the King told them these were all the treasures he possessed: God alone sent the crop-giving waters and the warmth of the sun: which are the real wealth of Ceylon. So these gentle souls took him back to prison, stripped him, bound him with chains, and building up the wall, left him to a lingering death — buried alive.

Though now free of his father, Kasyappa lived in fear of his brother's revenge: so with feverish haste he built himself a citadel on the top of Sigiriya, and lived there with his court. Eighteen years later Moggallana came against him with an army from India. Kasyappa, instead of remaining safely on top of Sigiriya, came down to fight his brother in the plains. The battle, though fierce, was undecided, till Kasyappa turning his elephant to go round a swamp, showed his back to the enemy. His people thought he was fleeing, and they broke and fled. The King, seeing the waves of troops rushing up to capture him, cut his throat, and fell dead.

Whereupon Moggallana reigned in peace. But Sigiriya was never again used as the capital, and disappeared from history shortly after this, swallowed up by the jungle-tide.

Rarely, I imagine, has a city risen so high and fallen so low in 15 short years.

The Rest-house keeper here, long ago, was a great sportsman. When we arrived he was mourning the loss of his pet goat.

"What happened?" I asked.

"Leopard swallowing, Master."

"What did you do?"

"Of course I am shooting leopard."

"What about your goat?"

"Also I am shooting him, inside of leopard!" he replied, cheerfully.

I love Sigiri — as it is usually called — dearly. Come with me to the top, taking tiffin and tea with us. A short walk past the tank takes us to the foot of the fortress. Slowly and gently we climb. Soon we are above the sea of waving jungle, and obtain a glorious view over the verdant forest-filled plain. Then, on the left, we come to the King's Bath, hewn out of the living rock. Close by we see the King's Seat, on which he sat to judge the people. It is rather like the Lion Throne at Mahabalipuram in South India. We rise higher, and enter the long narrow gallery, cut in the solid rock, with a parapet wall to our left of polished cement, as hard as rock itself. In the roof of the gallery are still some striking ancient Sinhalese paintings, full of life and colour. To prevent drought, every drop of precious rain water that fell on the hill was carefully accumulated in great tanks. Notice how the gallery is protected from rain.

At the further end, emerging from the narrow gallery, we look down on the ancient outworks, and notice a huge rock delicately poised on great stone sets, ready at a touch to be hurled down on foes attacking the main gate below. Finally we reach that puzzle of the ages — now solved. The historical records spoke of people ascending to the citadel on the very top, *"through the lion's mouth."* When two huge lion claws of cement were exhumed, it seemed clear that a great brick lion was once built here, and men used his open mouth as a gate. The picture shows the idea, as partially and prosaically restored to-day. From here you can ascend by light stairways to the citadel on the summit. Every yard of ground here is historic and noble, and affords wonderful evidence of the strenuous work done in a few years, which turned an inaccessible rock into an inexpugnable stronghold.

From the upper parts you may see great swarms of bees clinging to the rock below. Disturb them not: as did the party of His Royal Highness the Duke of Connaught, K.G., when he visited Sigiri long ago with his wife and daughter, then Princess Patricia.

The bees of Ceylon are well-described by Knox in his book, (of which my fine copy of the original edition of 1681 is before me as I write):—

Of bees, "there be three sorts. The first are the Meemasses, which are the right *English bees*. The second are the Bambaras, larger and of a brighter colour than our *English bees*. The third sort they call *Connameia,* signifying a blind bee. When they meet with any swarms of bees hanging on any tree, they will hold torches to make them drop; and so catch and carry them home. Which they boil and eat, and esteem excellent food."

At Sigiriya one sees mostly Bambaras — whose sting can be most unpleasant. The Veddahs love honey, and descend the cliffs by rickety bamboo ladders to rob the bees of their honey stored in clefts. Once a friend of mine told a jungle Veddah to find him some honey. The Veddah at once started on the task, darting to and fro through the jungle, looking up keenly. After twenty minutes he stopped, indicated a tree, and said, "In this tree, honey!" And there was. He had watched for bees with *full* sacs of honey flying home. Empty bees of course were going away from home in search of honey. Those bees he disregarded. It sounds easy. Try it, yourself! Personally I could rarely see a bee — much less the state of his belly!

Half-a-mile away from the Rest-house is the little hamlet of Sigiri, which is well worth a visit. Here you will see a primitive village in simple surroundings, and visualize what Mr. Parker has so well described. The life of such a villager is a hard life. The fields give but a scanty food-supply, which is precariously augmented by jungle food. The village cattle, lean and docile, tell the same story. The villager always has a passion for cattle; a survival of the old pastoral days, when cattle meant wealth, reminding one that *"pecuniary"* is derived from the Latin word *"pecus,"* or flock. The villager takes little thought for improving the breed. What served his ancestors suffices for him. These wiry little beasts, however, do heroic work in bullock-cart and plough assisted often by buffaloes.

Great is the sword and mighty is the pen,
But greater far the labouring ploughman's trade:
For on its oxen and its husbandmen
An Empire's strength is laid.

Once, a thousand years ago, what is now dense jungle round Sigiri was a tract of waving rice-fields, watered by a hundred tanks. And rice ought still to be the staple food of Ceylon, though in the jungle many are too poor to eat it regularly.

The terraced paddy-fields round Kandy and Badulla form lovely curves of light green, or rich yellow at time of harvest. The water is cunningly induced to irrigate every inch, not a drop being wasted. In the Low-country the tanks and *elas* feed the parched soil in flat fields. There are two crops of paddy each year if — there is enough water. The sun, happily, never fails. The *maha* (that is "great") crop is sown in July, August or September, according to altitude, and reaped in the following February or March. The *yala* crop is the short crop, being sown in April and reaped in July or August. In every operation the *goiya,* or cultivator, seeks the favour of Heaven, and from his astrologer ascertains the lucky day and hour for each operation. His methods thereafter are at least ten thousand years old; and some of his implements look even older. But, somehow, he grows rice. How much is grown in Ceylon is not known accurately, but some people say that Ceylon grows half of the rice consumed. Now, probably, it is less. Europeans, by the way, talk of curry and rice. The villager talks of *taking his rice.* With him the curry is usually a minus quantity. At the most it is a little dried fish, or a chillie *sambol.*

All through the jungle districts you will see patches burned down and roughly fenced in. These are called *chenas.* In the dry zone it is often impossible to grow enough rice, and the villager is too poor to buy it from traders. So he burns down a bit of jungle, waits for the rainy season, and then plants up "dry grains in the ashes," such as maize, millet, *kurakkan* and so forth. In due season his enclosure bears a scanty crop, which he guards anxiously, perched in a rickety erection of sticks and thatch in the Heath-Robinson style. In this he squats through dismal nights, armed with his gas-pipe muzzle-loader. My Lord the Elephant, the nimble deer, the long-tusked up-rooting wild pig, and other foes invade his piteous acre; which after one crop relapses again into jungle.

Government rages against this wasteful form of cultivation, which it seeks to control by the issue of chena permits. Prosecutions for unlawful *chena* cultivation are frequent in the Anuradhapura district. But it has gone on for centuries, is going, and will go on, till the jungle life gives place to ordered agriculture.

Which day, I pray, that I personally may never see. For the villager is a good fellow, courteous, brave, hospitable, and humorous, and in his quaint way extracts more than a little happiness in the face of many tribulations, of which drought, malaria, and the villager money-lender are the worst.

Before we leave Sigiri let me record its final claim to greatness. The Rest-house Keeper makes the best toast in Ceylon.

And here we end our visit to the Buried Cities recalling:—

Cities and Thrones and Powers
Last in Time's eye
Almost as long as flowers,
Which daily die.

CHAPTER XVII

THE CHINESE IN CEYLON.

[I am indebted for much of the information in this chapter to the learned writings of Mr. Edward W. Perera, Advocate and Antiquary, of Colombo.]

MOST people know that Ceylon has been wholly or in part ruled in times past from Lisbon, The Hague, Madras, and London. But not many, I imagine, realize that the Emperor of China once exercised suzerainty over Ceylon, and exacted tribute. It came to pass thus:—

After the Sinhalese glory departed from Polonnaruwa, leaving palaces forsaken, and watch-towers used as dens by wild beasts, in due course, a Sinhalese King, Sri Parakrama Bahu VI (1412-1467) reigned at Kotte (Cotta), some seven miles from modern Colombo. The classical name of this city was Jayawardhanapura. The traveller De Marignolli (*Circa* A.D. 1345) refers thus to Kotte: *"If we suppose Cain builded his city (Genesis IV:17) after the murder of Abel, this city of his is thought to have been where now is the city called Kota, Ceyllan, a place where I have been."*

This famous sovereign, Parakrama Bahu VI, virtually the last to reign over the whole of Lanka, had a picturesque career. He was the son of Vijaya Bahu VI (1400-1411). Then, in war-galleys, to Ceylon came the Chinese, who sacked Kotte and captured the King. His Queen with her little son escaped. In the resulting confusion the Minister Alakesvara seized the supreme power and sought to kill the heir. Soon after, however, the Minister was slain by the heir to the throne, who rose against him, and ascended the throne as Parakrama Bahu VI. Under him Kotte was gloriously embellished with a great palace of blue stone, many temples, and strong fortifications — of which, to-day, only a few stones remain. Here were well preserved the sacred relics of Buddha, in the Pas Mal Peya (*Five-storied Palace*), of whom many poets sang,

> *"There, in a palace of moonstone, strings of pearls hang from the palace eaves, and glittering gems shine upon the chatta of solid gold."*

Two small granite columns still remain to mark the spot where the sacred vessel of the God had been deposited. This King built also a Dalada Maligawa (*Temple of the Sacred Tooth*) in three stories in the form of a Crown, exceeding magnifical. "This epoch," writes Mr. Edward W. Perera, "saw in a marked degree the compromise between Hinduism and Buddhism which had existed in Ceylon from earliest times. This toleration sprang from two causes: the spirit of adaptability of Hinduism to changed conditions and alien ideals on the one hand, and on the other to the wisdom of the Buddhist hierarchs, who realized the peril to the Church in an attitude of avowed hostility to a faith which was favoured by the King, nobles, and even by the people."

The King caused to be made for the Tooth Relic "*a wonderful golden casket set with excellent gems, and encased it in another golden casket, which he encased in a third golden casket.*" He also built a spacious monastery for the Priests, with a great Ordination Chamber, where young priests were ceremoniously received into the Buddhist Church, and put on the yellow robe.

The choice of King Parakrama Bahu by the people of Ceylon was duly ratified by the Emperor of China, who claimed suzerainty over Lanka by reason of his capture of the late King. In Chinese Records there is an Imperial Edict confirming the election of King Parakrama Bahu. The suzerainty involved the payment of an yearly tribute to the Dragon Throne — tribute being first paid to the Celestial Envoys who brought the Imperial Edict from China to Ceylon about the year 1454. But when in 1459 the Chinese next came to exact tribute, they were sent away empty-handed; for the King of Lanka, in his strength, could now haughtily bid the Chinese junks depart; and they departed; and never came back again. Mr. Perera says:—

> *"This was the last time that the Imperial Chinese galleys swept our seas; but they were soon to be replaced by the keels of a Power far more formidable than the Manchu Tartars."*

The next foe to be repulsed was the King of Canara in South India, who in 1451 attacked Lanka with a large fleet and army, but was severely defeated. A *casus belli* arose later, and

Parakrama in turn invaded Canara (now called Mysore) and inflicted heavy losses on the Canarese. His army returned with much spoil. Gradually King Parakrama's swelling bounds increased, till he was King of all Lanka. He was the first King to place on a sound basis the taxation of the kingdom; and he generously endowed the Buddhist Church, granting for the upkeep of the Dalada Maligawa all land dues and port dues; and in general he set up standards of efficient government.

It is worthy of note that this King subdued both the King of Candy, and the King of Jaffna, Arya Chakkrawarti. The latter, with his Tamil chieftains, called Vanniyars, had long defied successive Sinhalese rulers, and finally proclaimed himself Emperor of Ceylon. Parakrama Bahu, incensed at this affront, decided that *"There should no longer be two Kings in Ceylon."* He sent his army, under a great Captain, Sapumal Kumara — a terrifying warrior, riding (according to Valentyn) *"a blue horse with a green mane."* After hard fighting and great slaughter Jaffna was captured after a brave resistance; the monarch driven out; and the Sinhalese troops returned in triumph to Kotte.

A poem, *The Selalihini Sandesa,* gives a vivid picture of this war. One verse may be roughly interpreted thus, on the lines of the translation made by Mr. H. C. P. Bell, C.C.S. :—

"Behold the conquering Sappoe comes from Jaffna in the North,
Around him grouped a mighty host, that proved its martial worth;
Above, the snow-white chatta gleams, its gems all glittering bright;
Below, He on his sable steed recalls the Sun God's light."

One gathers this famous war-horse was a blue-black roan. As to the green mane I can offer no explanation, except dye.

In the 55th year of his reign this great sovereign, Sri Parakrama Bahu VI, slept with his fathers, and his grandson reigned in his stead. For nearly a hundred years longer this kingdom continued; and then it fell, under the impact of disintegrating forces, and continued attacks of the Portuguese.

His was the last Golden Age of wide Sinhalese sovereignty, that preceded the dark era of Portuguese sway over the sea-coasts of Lanka. Valentyn and Da Couto, both Portuguese, wrote at length on this period. The Sinhalese Chronicle of this period is called *The Rajavaliya.* All these works make most interesting reading. Thus it was in the 16th Century that the Sinhalese Dynasty, founded in 543 B.C., lost dominion over the Maritime Provinces of Lanka. Thereafter, Sinhalese power was centred in Kandy.

Knox's name, *Chingulays,* for the Sinhalese comes from the Chinese, or Chins. They called Ceylon, *Chingula,* since they claimed suzerainty. Sinhalese, of course, comes from *Sinha,* meaning Lion. The Chinese called Ceylon SH
TSZ
KWO

In the Colombo Museum is a most interesting testimony of the Chinese in Ceylon. — the large trilingual stone facing the statue of Parakrama Bahu. I wish I could deal with this more fully, but that must be reserved for some future occasion, owing to lack of space.

Such, in variegated outline, is the long History of Ceylon.

Is it not written :—

Arise, shine; for thy light is come, and the glory of God is risen upon thee.

Nations shall come to thy light. And kings to the brightness of thy rising.

Lift up thine eyes round about, and see: they all gather themselves together. They come to thee.

Violence shall no more be heard in thy land.

Then thou shalt see and be radiant, and thy heart shall thrill and be enlarged: Because the abundance of the sea shall be turned unto thee, the wealth of the nations shall be thine.

Thy gates shall be open continually. They shall not be shut day or night.

A little one shall become a thousand, and a small one a strong nation.

God will hasten it in his time.

CHAPTER XVIII

RELIGIONS OF CEYLON

EVERY visitor should know something about the principal religions of Ceylon, as otherwise they cannot appreciate much that they will see. The Registrar-General has kindly furnished me with the figures below. I am indebted to three friends at the Colombo Bar, Mr. K. S. Vagiswara Aiyar, Mr. A. W. H. Abeysundere, and Mr. M. Maharoof, who have kindly written a brief outline of Hinduism, Buddhism and Mohammedanism, respectively, at my request.

Religion.	Estimated population 1931	Estimated population 1936.
Buddhists	3,267,457	3,467,200
Hindus	1,158,522	1,229,300
Christians	523,066	555,000
Muslims	356,888	378,700
Others	938	1,000
Total (Ceylon)	5,306,871	5,631,200

* The figures are based on the religion distribution at the Census of 1921.

III.—Number of Buddhist Monks.

No. of Buddhist Monks at the Census of 1921 was 9,666.

No. of Bhikshus registered under Ordinance No. 9 of 1931 up to the end of the year 1936.	(a) Upasampada—8049 (b) Samanera —5815.

N.B.—The total of Upasampada and Samanera Bhikshus does not represent the total number of Buddhist Monks, as the same Bhikshu may have been registered once as Samanera and again as Upasampada, and the number of Monks who died or left the robes is not available.

IV.—No. of Churches in Ceylon by Denomination.

Denomination.			No. of Churches, Chapels, etc. in Ceylon in 1936.
American Church Mission	...	...	42
Baptist Missionary Society	...	...	29
Ceylon and India General Mission		...	6
Church of Ceylon (formerly known as Church of England in Ceylon)	...	...	228
Church of Scotland	...	...	2
Dutch Reformed Church	...	...	9
Friends' Mission ...	...	...	6
Independent Catholic Mission	...	...	1
Methodist Mission	...	...	180
Roman Catholic Church	...	...	803
Salvation Army	...	...	60
Seventh Day Adventists' Mission		...	6
		Total	1,372

The first mention of Christianity in Ceylon comes from Sopater, a Greek merchant, who came to Ceylon from Abyssinia in a Persian ship, which anchored in some harbour. That happened about A.D. 525, and it would appear that a Persian Christian Colony had existed from early times. A Nestorian Cross of this community is in the Anuradhapura Museum. Probably Christianity came from South India originally to Ceylon, as St. Thomas, the Apostle, by tradition preached the Gospel in about the year A.D. 74 and was martyred at St. Thomas' Mount near Madras. The first Christian King of Ceylon was called Don Juan Dharmapala, who gave over his crown to the King of Portugal, and made Portuguese the Court language. I might mention that King Raja Singha spoke Portuguese fluently.

The Roman Catholic Communion in Ceylon, by tradition, dates from very early time. Long ago, at the Centenary in 1894 of Jaffna Cathedral, Monsignor Zaleski, Delegate Apostolic said :—

"Catholics of Jaffna! Yours is a glorious story. You were they say, the first to bend your knees before our Lord Jesus Christ, as according to an old and venerable tradition, one of the three kings who came to the humble stable of Bethlehem to adore the child Jesus, Gaspar Peria-Perumal, was a king of Jaffna. Thence he returned to Jaffna, joined afterwards the Holy

The Travels of Fa-Hien

Buddha Tossing the Elephant Over the Wall

The Travels of Fa-Hien

Division of Buddha's Relics

By courtesy *The Ceylon Tea Propaganda Board.*

Kandyan Dancers.

Apostle St. Thomas on his arrival in India, and was baptized by him, ordained a priest and consecrated Bishop, died the death of a martyr together with this Apostle St. Thomas, and both were buried in the same grave."

2

We will take the three religions in the order in which they came to Ceylon.

HINDUISM

THE Hindus of Ceylon consist of two groups; Ceylon Tamils, and Indians living in Ceylon. Of those two the majority are Tamils by race. In our sketch of Hinduism in Ceylon more attention will, therefore, be paid to a consideration of Hinduism as interpreted and followed by Tamils.

Now what constitutes Hinduism? Alexander the Great fought the ill-fated Indian King, Porus, in the valley of the *Sindhu* — the river Indus — and the Greeks thereafter chose to label the Indians as *Hindu;* the letter *H* being a variant of *S.* Since then the West has identified the people of India, on the religious side of their life, by the term Hindu; and Hinduism in the phraseology of the West includes innumerable shades of faiths and doctrines covered by monotheism, pantheism, agnosticism, atheism, polytheism and fetishism. To the Indians it is his *Matham,* (his opinion). Each man or group of men is free to have his opinion in matters religious, as long as he subscribes to certain fundamentals, presently to be mentioned. He is free to have his own way of thought and belief, and yet have the right to be in the Hindu fold. As Prof. Radhakrishna observes truly, "while it gives absolute liberty in the world of thought, it enjoys a strict code of practice. The theist and the atheist, the sceptic and the agnostic, may all be Hindus, if they accept the Hindu system of culture and life."

The principles and tenets of Hinduism are embedded in the four *Vedas, viz., Rig, Yajur, Sama* and *Atharva.* They are the *Sruti* of the Hindu Code — "*what was heard or revealed.*" Of equal sanctity are the *Brahmanas* and the *Upanishads* which form the *Smriti* — "*what was remembered.*" The *Smritis* are commentaries on the *Vedas:* and, in the absence of writing at the time, had to be stored in the memory of men and orally transmitted to successive generations of disciples. As the *Brahmanas* and the *Upanishads* were learnt by the pupil after a course in the *Vedas,* they are commonly referred to as *Vedanta — what is at the end of the Vedas.*

The essence of higher Hinduism lies hidden in these sacred books. Their cardinal principle is the belief in the one-ness of being. Everything that exists is *Brahma,* the supreme spirit which animates the whole world of man and beast and matter. By a process of further introspection, Vedic Society evolved the idea of the well-known triad of Gods. *Brahma* is the supreme manifestation of the universal spirit in its creative aspect. *Vishnu* is the manifestation of the power of preservation and protection. And *Siva* symbolises the process of dissolution as well as reproduction, the force which controls the unending cycle of birth, death, and re-birth. The tendency of the Hindu mind was gradually to concentrate more and more on the latter two manifestations of Divine Purpose, *Vishnu* and *Siva.* The far-seeing intellect and imagination of the Brahman priesthood wove into the web of Indian religious thought female consorts to the three forces of the Spirit Immortal. Out of the fertile and purposeful imagination of Brahmans arose *Sarasvathi,* the consort of Brahama and the Goddess of learning; *Laksmi* the consort of Vishnu and the Goddess of prosperity; and *Uma,* the consort of Siva, variously known as *Parvati, Bhavani, Durga,* or *Kali.*

All Hindus subscribe to the doctrines of *Karma* and the transmigration of souls; and among the beliefs prevalent among the masses are the institution of caste, with the Brahman at the head, and the veneration of the cow, the embodiment of all that is useful to man in his every-day life.

Coming to Hinduism of the Tamils in Ceylon, we have it on the authority of the *Ramayana* that Ravana, the legendary King of Lanka, was a *Sivite, i.e.,* one who belonged to that section of the society which had chosen *Siva* for their exclusive meditation and intimate realisation.

Through the whole of the *Siva Sidhantha* and the hymns of the great Tamil sages runs one central idea permeating the rest — the quest after the unrealisable, unknowable, inexpressible *Siva.* There is no image of Him whose name is *Great Glory.* But, from this idea of *Siva* the formless, a conception of *Siva's* form as the *linga* somehow or other has grown. Learned men explain the adoption of this symbol for a god of whom 'there is no image' as an attempt to express the inexpressible. Read in this light, the phallic emblem of the *linga* — so essential a feature of *Sivite* worship — becomes meaningful to those who may care to appreciate and understand the *lingam* in a Siva temple.

The history of Indian religious thought from the beginning of the Christian Era has been the development of the Krishna cult of *bhakti,* or love, among the *Vishnuvites,* and of *Siva bhakti* among the Tamils of South India and Ceylon. The famous singers and seers of the Tamil land beginning with *Manikka-Vasagar* were inspired and fortified by their intense *bhakti,* their love for and faith in *Siva. Thiru Vasagam* ("the sacred utterances" of Manikka-Vasagar) is easily the best known in Tamil sacred literature, and is full of the intense religious feeling and fervour of the Siva devotee. Sings the sage Manikka-Vasagar — *"Mal (Vishnu), Ayan, all the gods and sciences divine His essence cannot pierce. This Being rare drew near to me;*
In love he thrilled my soul."

The Sivite fervour of Manikka-Vasagar transmuted even the repellent aspects of Siva into the purposes of Divine Grace. Siva is *He who wears the Chaplet of skulls,*
the *maniac* with

A dancing snake his jewel, a tiger-skin his robe,
A form with ashes smeared he wears.

If the visitor to Ceylon will keep this aspect of Siva worship in his mind, the familiar sight of the Hindu mendicant smeared with holy ash, (*Thiru-niru*) with a string of beads (*Rudrak-shara*) dangling from his neck, his long-grown hair matted and pleated into a tuft crowning his head, with perhaps an ill-seasoned leopard-skin flung across his body, commanding, if not winning the obeisance of a Sivite crowd, may become intelligible.

We may now make a passing reference to some of the Hindu shrines in Ceylon. Adam's Peak is to Hindus their *Sivan-oli-padam.*

The hollow on the Peak, according to tradition, was blessed by the touch of Siva's feet.

The Sivites along with the rest of the Hindus believe that the present age in the cycle of time is *Kali-Yuga;* and the six-faced *Subramanaya*, the son of Siva, is *Kali Yuga Varathar*, the supreme power that controls the present age. No wonder then that more prominence is given by the Sivites of South India and Ceylon to the worship of the Lord that controls the age. Subramanaya, whom the Tamils love to worship as *Skanda* or *Kathira* or *Murugan*, ultimately destroyed *Sura*, the scourge of the Gods. In the Veddah village of *Kathira-gama*, in the wilds of Badulla District, tradition has housed *Kathira-esa* from time immemorial; and in the month of Adi, (July-August), on full moon day is held the *Adi-Vel* festival, so common in the worship of the Lord Subramanaya in Tamil land.

Subramanaya's weapon of war, with which he slew *Sura*, is the spear-shaped *Vel*. And this is the origin and meaning of *Adi-Vel*. According to tradition Valli, the Veddah damsel, lived in the forest where the shrine of Kathira-gama stands to-day. And when, in accordance with custom, she was keeping guard on the *tena* plantation, Murugan won the love of the Veddah damsel and married her. Dutugemunu, the Sinhalese Buddhist King who reigned in Ceylon nearly 2,000 years ago, is believed to have erected the temple, which enshrines the veiled mystery of the casket and the subsidiary one in honour of *Valli*, Murugan's consort. Farther still in the wilderness, on the rocky summit of the mountain, is the *Vel* symbolical of God's protection and power. The Vel festival at Kathira-gama is bereft of pomp and rituals. The casket of mystery is first taken on the back of a caparisoned elephant in a procession round the shrine. But if the festival lacks rituals and ceremonies, it is impregnated with the fervour and devotion of the thousands of pilgrims who flock together from diverse parts of Ceylon and India.

The *Vel festival* of Colombo had its beginnings in the annual pilgrimages on foot, which the devotees of the two Kathirasan temples in Sea Street organized to this Holy Shrine at Kathira-gama. But the Nattukottai Chettiar community (who owned these temples and to whom business is second nature) devised a more practical proposition, when they erected two temples at Wellawatte and Bambalapitiya, and organised the Vel Festival of Colombo. The silver chariot, carries *Shunmukka-Vel-Ayduha* from Sea Street to the Temple in Wellawatte or Bambalapitiya, in turn each year; and the chariot returns, after the customary ceremonies, to Sea Street through a surging mass of worshippers and sight-seers.

The visitor to Ceylon will be interested in the Siva-temple at Kochikadai in Colombo, erected by the munificence and devotion of a Sivite family of Colombo. The late Sir Ponnambalam Ramanathan, a distinguished son of this illustrious family, undertook the task of re-erecting the temple on the principles of real South Indian temple architecture; and, even in its incomplete state, the Sivan Kovil is a credit to Ceylon from the point of view of South Indian Art.

There are innumerable other Hindu shrines in Ceylon, particularly in the Northern Province where the Tamils predominate. They exercise varying influences and have varying origins. The tomb where a Sanyasin (or *respected person*) lies in *samadhi* has very often developed into a place of worship, and the departed leader is deified by the masses. Our sketch will, however, be incomplete without a reference to a peculiar feature of religious life among the people of Ceylon, namely, the presence of *Vishnu* and other Hindu deities in *Buddhist Vihares* or temples.

Tradition has it that Wijaya, the first Aryan invader of Ceylon, was obliged to go to India to find a consort of equal social status. From the beginning of Ceylon history, Sinhalese Buddhist Kings very often married Indian Hindu Princesses. The Hindu Queen in the Royal Household was perhaps responsible for the erection in the *Vihare* of a shrine where she might worship *Vishnu*, or such other Hindu deity, in whom she had faith. It has also to be remembered that the Buddha himself was born a Hindu; lived a Hindu; and died a Hindu; and that Buddhists believe that *Vishnu* is one of the Devas or Super Human Beings who influence affairs. The visitor to the famous *Vihare* at Dambulla will be impressed with the statue of *Vishnu,* surrounded by other Devas; and the story will be related to him that the *Vihare* was built with the assistance of *Vishnu,* the Supreme Deva.

We may conclude by quoting the too familiar prayer, which puts in a nut-shell the Hindu's outlook on his own faith and the faith of others.

Rains which fall from skies all over, all flow into one sea.
Prayers, which man offers to Gods of diverse names,
All reach the God of All.

BUDDHISM.

Buddhism, whose adherents constitute nearly two-thirds of Ceylon's population, was introduced from India by the Prince-monk Mahinda, who was a son of the Indian Emperor Asoka. This monk settled down in Ceylon. He lived at Mihintale, which is eight miles east of Anuradhapura. The traditional date of the introduction of Buddhism to Ceylon is 307 B.C., but scholars are of the opinion that it is 247 B.C.

The teaching of the Buddha is called Buddhism. The "Buddha" means the "Fully Enlightened One." Anyone can become a Buddha by reaching the highest state of perfection through self-purification. There have been many Buddhas in the past æons. The last of them was the Buddha known as Gautama.

The Buddha Gautama was an Indian prince born in 623 B.C. at Kapilavastu on the borders of modern Nepal. His full name was Siddhartha Gautama. He was married to Princess Yasodara and had a son called Rahula. When Prince Siddhartha was 29 years of age, he renounced the world and became a hermit. At the age of 35 he attained Buddhahood while meditating under a Pipal-tree (*ficus religiosa*) on the bank of the river Neranjara in Gaya. He died at the age of 80 at Kusinara.

Tradition records that the Buddha Gautama visited Ceylon on three occasions. He is said to have come to Mahiyangana in Eastern Ceylon, Nagadhipa (modern Jaffna) in Northern Ceylon, and Kelaniya in Western Ceylon, where there is a famous temple. During the last visit he is said to have gone to the hill of Samantakuta (modern Adam's Peak) and left his footprint on the peak. Hence the Sinhalese Buddhists call this peak Sri Padha, which means "Exalted Foot."

The variety of tree, under which the Buddha Gautama attained Buddhahood, is called Bodhi-tree, or in its abbreviated form Bo-tree. ("*Bodhi*" means "Wisdom"). A branch of the sacred Bo-tree at Gaya was brought to Ceylon by the Princess-nun Sanghamitta not long after the arrival in Ceylon of her brother, the Prince-monk Mahinda. It was planted at Anuradhapura, where it still exists after surviving the vicissitudes of over 2,000 years.

The Buddhists of Ceylon believe that the Buddha Gautama was born, attained Buddhahood, and died on the full moon day of the Sinhalese lunar month of Wesak (month of May). Every

Buddhist home in Ceylon is gaily decorated and brightly illuminated on Wesak Day in commemoration of these three events.

Buddhism is an exposition of the Law of the Cosmic Order. It propounds the "Four Noble Truths," namely, (1) Suffering. (2) Origin of Suffering, (3) Extinction of Suffering, (4) Path leading to the Extinction of Suffering.

Suffering is the insatiableness of desires appertaining to the five aggregates of existence composed of bodily form, feeling, perception, (mental) formations, and consciousness. The Origin of Suffering is Craving caused by greed, ill-will, and ignorance. The Extinction of Suffering is the annihilation of Craving. The "Noble Eightfold Path" leads to the Extinction of Suffering.

The "Noble Eightfold Path" is a *Via Media*, which avoids the two extremes of self-indulgence and self-mortification. It consists of (1) Right Understanding, (2) Right Aspiration, (both of which constitute Wisdom), (3) Right Speech, (4) Right Action, (5) Right Means of Livelihood, (the three of which constitute Morality), (6) Right Effort, (7) Right Attentiveness, (8) Right Meditation, (the three of which constitute Concentration). The consummation of all these eight is the deliverance from greed, ill-will, and ignorance.

When Craving is annihilated by treading the "Noble Eightfold Path," rebirth is exhausted and the state of "Nibbana" is reached. "Nibbana" is the "*summum bonum*" of Buddhism.

ISLAM.

There are about 378,700 people in Ceylon who profess Islam as their religion. They belong to various races—(a) The Ceylon Moors who form the majority, and who are the descendants of the Arabs who settled down in the Island during the time of the early Sinhalese kings; (b) the Malays, whose association with the Island began in the Dutch era, and (c) Indians, who have wide business interests in the country. In spite of this diversity of races they are linked together into one great Brotherhood by the ties of their religion.

One of the four great religions of the world, Islam is remarkably free from dogma and theology. The essence of its ethical principles is indicated in the word "Islam" itself which in its primary sense means "to be tranquil, at rest, patient and resigned, to have arrived at perfect peace." In its secondary sense it means surrendering oneself without doubt or questioning to Him who has created all.

There are five duties which are enjoined on all Muslims.

(a) Bearing witness that there is but one God, and Muhammad is the Prophet of God.

(b) Reciting the daily prayers.

(c) Giving the legal alms.

(d) Observing the Ramazan, or the month's fast.

(e) Making the pilgrimage to Mecca one in a lifetime.

The great Civil, Criminal and Moral, Law Code of the Muslims is the "Koran," which is accepted by them as the inspired Word of God. Written in the purest Arabic dialect, it is the source of inspiration to all Muslims, and guides them in all their activities.

Muslims are divided into two main schools of thought—the Sunnis, and the Shiahs. The former acknowledge the first four Khalifahs to have been the rightful successors of Muhammad, and belong to one of the four schools of Jurisprudence founded by Imam Abu Hanifah, Imam Ash Shafi, Imam Malik or Imam Ahmad Ibn Hambal. The Shiahs, however, maintain that Ali, the first cousin of Muhammad and the husband of his daughter Fatimah, was the first legitimate Imam or Khalifa or successor to the Prophet. The majority of Muslims in Ceylon belong to the Sunni school of thought.

Recognising, as it does, the universal brotherhood of man, Islam has been a great unifying force in the world and in the words of Bernard Shaw "*is the only religion which appears to possess that assimilating capability to the changing phases of existence which can make itself appeal to every age.*"

The Mosques of Ceylon are beautiful buildings, and in Colombo are easily accessible—one, for example, is opposite Maradana Station, and another stands near the Town Hall in the Cinnamon Gardens. On the road to Galle a beautiful Mosque should be visited at Beruwela, where many Muslims reside.

Here endeth the Chapter on the Religions of Ceylon.

As all rivers flow to the sea,
So should each Religion lead men to God.

This is the end of the End of this little Book. I feel there is still so much to say: so little said. I have just tried to sketch a faint Ceylonian outline, which you will fill in and colour to your taste. I close with five Sinhalese proverbs of comfort:

Can a single tree make an orchard?

My critics may (justly) be severe:—But—

Will the mountain grow smaller because the dog barked at it?

And again:

Are the five fingers of the same length?

In Ceylon religion was the inspiration:

Even a butterfly seeks the Peak of religious expression.

Finally:

The gift of a gift is the supreme gift.

This is my little gift to you.

—C. Brooke Elliott.